MW00851671

Table of Contents

Introduction

Congratulations on your decision to take the GRE, and welcome to the Accepted, Inc. *Guide to Conquering the GRE*, which contains everything you need to know to do your best and nothing that won't help. By this point in your academic career, you know your own test-taking strategies and style. Because you know best how you learn material, this guide does not offer gimmicks or tricks. Instead, we aim to educate you about what will be on the GRE so that you can prepare yourself. This guide includes information about how the test is structured and scored, detailed explanations of the question formats and content for each of the three sections of the GRE, and two exams' worth of practice questions so that you can hone your approach and walk into the test confident in your readiness.

About the GRE

The GRE – the Graduate Record Exam – is written, administered, and scored by a private company, Educational Testing Service (ETS). The GRE is intended to distill your critical reasoning abilities into a set of numbers; however, as is the case with all standardized tests, it better reflects your ability to prepare for a standardized test. The test was overhauled by the ETS in 2011, which changed the GRE's format and content. Keep this in mind – things you may have heard about the GRE might no longer be relevant, and many online resources are not yet up to date. Use the information in this guide and the resources that we suggest to find current, accurate information about the test that you'll be taking.

What Does the GRE Cover?

The GRE has three section types: Analytic Writing (comprised of two essay prompts), Verbal Reasoning (which includes sentence completion and reading comprehension questions), and Quantitative Reasoning (which is comprised of math questions). Each of these sections is covered in a separate chapter in this guide. Here is a general overview of each:

Analytic Writing – You will write one essay which develops an argument regarding a given issue and one essay that analyzes another argument given in the prompt. The test allows you 30 minutes for each, and you do not see the second essay prompt until you have submitted your first essay. Your essays will be typed in a given text box, though you can use scratch paper to organize your thoughts. Each essay will be scored between 0 and 6 based on the clarity of your reasoning and the quality of your writing, and the two scores will be averaged together to create your section score.

Verbal Reasoning – You will have two multiple choice sections of twenty verbal questions. These 30 minute sections will test your vocabulary and reasoning skills with sentence completion questions, and your reading comprehension level with questions about the content of dull and obfuscated passages. Grammar will not be tested at all. You may also take a third, experimental verbal section, but it will not be scored.

Quantitative Reasoning – You will take two 20-question math sections. Each 30-minute math section will cover the same mathematical concepts from the SAT: geometry, algebra, patterns, mathematical definitions, fractions, and exponents. The

[handwritten margin note: ＊ Render obscure, unclear, or unintelligible]

[handwritten note near "obfuscated": ＄]

math does not test beyond what you learned in the 10th grade. However, the questions are asked in a way that can be tricky if you aren't familiar with the style they are asked in (which we'll cover in this guide). You are not allowed your own calculator, but one is provided on the screen that can handle addition, subtraction, multiplication, division, and square roots. Don't forget that the GRE is a reasoning test, not an arithmetic test. You may also take a third, experimental math section, but it will not be scored.

How is the test structured?

When you take the electronic GRE, your schedule will look like this:

1 hour	Analytic Writing	Two back-to-back 30 minute essays
30 or 35 minutes	Verbal OR Quantitative Reasoning	One 20-question section
30 or 35 minutes	Verbal OR Quantitative Reasoning	One 20-question section
10 Minute Break		
30 or 35 minutes	Verbal OR Quantitative Reasoning	One 20-question section
30 or 35 minutes	Verbal OR Quantitative Reasoning	One 20-question section
30 or 35 minutes	Verbal OR Quantitative Reasoning	One 20-question section

Two of the short sections will be Verbal Reasoning (30 minutes) and two will be Quantitative Reasoning (35 minutes). One short section will be an experimental or research section, and it may have either verbal or math questions. Experimental sections occur randomly and could be any section during the test; you will **not** be notified which section will not be scored. Research sections are given as the final section and you will be notified that it is a research section, even though it does not affect your score. Your test will contain either an experimental or a research section, not both, and you will not know which one you had until the last section. Just answer each section like it will be scored.

You can take the GRE in the morning or the afternoon, whichever appeals to you. It will take 3 hours and 45 minutes. You can find dates, and register to take the exam, at: http://www.ets.org/gre.

While the GRE is a computer-based test (CBT), in some parts of the world you may take a paper GRE; if that is the case for you, you can still use this guide because the question content is identical. Just ignore the notes about computer adaptivity and test navigation, and note that the Verbal and Quantitative Reasoning sections of the paper-based exam are 25 questions rather than 20. In general, most people who take the GRE take the test on a computer at a designated testing center.

How is the test scored?

Section Adaptivity
Before August 2011, the difficulty level of each question on the GRE adapted based on your successfully answering the previous question. Now the difficulty level only adjusts at the section level. Therefore, the difficulty of your second Verbal and second Quantitative section will vary based on your score to the first Verbal or Quantitative section. The first section of each type will always contain questions considered medium-difficulty. The section types are evaluated independently, so your success on a Verbal section will not affect the difficulty of your next Quantitative section, and vice versa.

How does ETS rate the difficulty level of a question? This is based on what percentage of test-takers answer similar questions correctly in the research and experimental sections of prior tests. If half of test-takers ace a question, that question is considered to be medium-level difficulty. Questions missed by more than half of test-takers are the ones chosen as higher-difficulty questions on subsequent tests.

You need to realize that **DIFFICULTY IS SUBJECTIVE**. What ETS considers a high-difficulty math concept may be a breeze for you, because you had a great algebra teacher and still remember the properties of exponents. Also, working through this guide will give you such an edge concerning different "tricks" of the GRE that you will have trouble distinguishing between what the test designers consider easy and hard questions. Conversely, we all sometimes get stuck on as easy question or make a mistake because we are rushing through something that we actually know how to do. Therefore, **do not** waste time or energy trying to divine your score on Section 1 based on how difficult you perceive Section 3 to be. On the GRE, your goal is to live in the now. Focus only on the section right in front of you.

Verbal and Quantitative Scoring
Each section is scored separately. Verbal and Quantitative Reasoning are each given a score between 130 and 170. The awesome thing about taking the GRE on a computer is that your Verbal and Quantitative Reasoning scores are displayed immediately after you finish, so your Analytic Writing score is the only one you have to wait to find out. Note that you can miss one or two questions on each section and still receive a perfect score, because the raw section scores are processed in relation to how everyone else taking this particular GRE performed. This gentle curve gives you some leeway and should help alleviate some of your exam stress.

The Verbal and Quantitative raw section scores are based simply on the number of questions you answered correctly and the difficulty level of those questions. Within a section, all questions are worth the same number of points, so feel free to skip around and answer the questions that you are comfortable with first. Unlike the SAT, **you do NOT lose points for answering a question wrong on the GRE.** You can take advantage of this by guessing answers on any questions that you have not completed once your section time is almost up. You should never leave a question unanswered.

Essay Scoring

The Analytic Essays are each scored twice. The ETS has begun using electronic grading algorithms to obtain the second grader's score, but at least one of your graders for each essay will be a living, breathing human. Ah, the brave new world of artificial intelligence! The ETS explains the process thusly: your essays will first be rated by experienced human graders (you'll have a different grader for each of your two essays). The essays will then be graded by the electronic program. If the electronic score is more than a point different from the first score, then another person will review the essay, and the two human-given scores will be averaged into a final score. If the first grader and the electronic score are within one point, then the first human-given score is the final score for that essay. To obtain your overall Analytic Writing section score, the two final scores for each essay are averaged together. This final score will be rounded to the nearest half-point on the scale from 0-6. In the Analytic Writing section chapter of this guide, we will further explore what graders, both human and electronic, look for when scoring your essays.

The Score Report

Each of your three section type scores are given separately, so a sample score report might read:

> Verbal Reasoning: 165
> Quantitative Reasoning: 157
> Analytic Reasoning: 5.0

One final note on GRE scoring: when you receive your score report, you will also be told which percentile you scored in each section. These percentiles reflect aggregated scores over several recent years. For example, if your Quantitative Reasoning percentile is given as 75%, that means that you performed better than 75% of people who have recently taken the GRE (the 75% who didn't read this *Guide to Conquering the GRE*). These percentile scores will not be reported to the graduate programs who receive your scores, only to you.

How to use this guide

This guide was written for you to use flexibly: you can study the Verbal section first if you want, or start with Quantitative Reasoning or Analytical Writing. The practice test sections are organized by subject, so you can take all of the Verbal test sections at once if you'd like, or alternate section types to mimic a real GRE. However, the guide is optimal if you use each section in this order:

1. **Strategy**: First, you should read through the Strategy chapters to familiarize yourself with the types of questions asked on the GRE and to review concepts. The Strategy chapters give general approaches that work for each section and cover the common question types. Each chapter has examples and includes practice questions which you can use to test your understanding as you proceed.

2. **Practice**: Once you've reviewed the Strategy chapter for a test section type, you can work through the problems in the Practice chapter for that type. You can read all the Strategy chapters first and then work all the problems or attack one test section at a time.

3. **Scoring and review**: After you have gone through the practice problems for a section, check your answers at the back of the Practice chapter. The answers given for the practice questions are very in-depth, and go heavily into strategy and content review. Some minor formulas and examples which may not be covered in the Strategy chapters are presented here.

4. **Preparing for the electronic test**: If you will be taking the GRE on a computer at a testing center (which you'll confirm when you register), you should review Appendix A so that you are comfortable with the way you will be navigating the electronic GRE.

5. **Optional additional practice**: If you have time, you can check out some of the additional resources given in Appendix B (aptly titled "Free Additional Resources"). Included are websites where you can download GRE test simulators if you would like to practice taking the GRE electronically. We recommend that you do not do this before first fully reviewing the material.

It's important not to over-prepare to the point that you burn out on this material. Cut yourself some slack as you practice, and remember that on test day your score will be curved; missing a few questions is no reason to panic. Also, you will not be surprised by anything on the test; and after reading this guide, where we'll cover all the likely question types and ways to handle them, you will definitely be prepared!

Chapter 1: Verbal Reasoning

Each Verbal Reasoning section on your test will have 20 questions and a time limit of 30 minutes. The Verbal Reasoning sections will have a mix of question types. It's important to check the directions for each question type as you encounter it; some questions will require you to select one answer choice, others require two answer choice selections, and some specify that you select "all that apply." This chapter will cover all the question types used on recent GRE exams, but remember to check the directions on your exam to make sure that you answer in the right way. Losing points for failing to read the directions is painful; don't let it happen to you!

Structure of the Verbal Reasoning Sections

There are three main question types in these sections: Sentence Equivalence, Text Completion, and Reading Comprehension. Sentence Equivalence questions give a sentence with one word missing, and a set of answer choices from which you select the **two** words which best fit in the blank. Text Completion questions will give you a block of text consisting of a one to five sentences, with several words missing. You will have a different set of answer choices for each blank in the text. Reading Comprehension questions will give you a short passage and ask you questions about the structure, argument, and tone of the passage. Each Verbal Reasoning section of the test will have a mix of these question types, in no particular order.

For each of these question types, you'll use similar strategies. You'll need to read carefully and think about what a sentence is actually saying. The strategy in this chapter emphasizes understanding the meaning of a sentence or text. Verbal Reasoning questions are designed to test your ability to understand the written word, and there are not tricks to get around this. During this section, we'll look at how relying on tricks and shortcuts can land you right into the trap of wrong answer choices, as well as how to best avoid these traps.

As you navigate through a Verbal Reasoning section on the GRE, you will be able to skip over questions and go back to them later. Keep this in mind: you can do your favorite type of question first to snag the points you feel confident about gaining, and then go back to do whichever type of question you feel trips you up. Remember that all questions within a section are worth the same amount of points, so there's no reason not to work through a section in the order that suits you. Take a moment to be very happy about this – before 2011, test-takers had to answer each question in the order it was given.

SENTENCE EQUIVALENCE

About one-third of the questions in the GRE Verbal Reasoning sections will be Sentence Equivalence questions. You are given a sentence with one word missing, and the answer choices are six possible words that might go in that blank. Many people mistakenly think that this is a vocabulary test, which is not true. Understanding a large percentage of the words used in these questions helps you, but these questions are testing your ability to read a sentence and understand its meaning despite a missing word. They are testing your cognitive ability to fill in the gaps, which is a great higher-order thinking skill. Don't be thrown by big words; you'll almost always be able to understand the sentence and enough of the answer choices to answer correctly, even if you do not recognize all of the words in the question.

Warning: Sentence Equivalence questions look similar to the shorter of the Text Completion questions, except that for Sentence Equivalence questions you will always need to select TWO answer choices.

READ THE DIRECTIONS to ensure that you are picking enough answers.

Sentence Equivalence questions look like this:

Directions: Select the two answer choices that, when used to complete the sentence, fit the meaning of the sentence as a whole and produce completed sentences that are alike in meaning.

His ---- style of speaking became a problem when others found him terse and rude.
   a) Laconic
   b) Erudite
   c) Flowery
   d) Baroque
   e) Succinct
   f) Droll

Note that the directions tell you to choose the two words which, when substituted into the sentence blank, produce sentences which are *alike in meaning*. Therefore, the correct answers have two criteria: they must each make sense in the sentence, and they must create two sentences which have the same underlying meaning.

Unfortunately, you can't just scan the answer choices for two synonyms and select those – ETS thought of this strategy, and they will use it against you to create trick solutions. For example, in our example sentence above, "flowery" and "baroque" are similar styles of speaking – both mean that the guy in this sentence gives wordy, poetic speeches. However, c) and d) are not the correct answers because they do not fit the underlying meaning of the sentence.

Another strategy that seems intuitive is to read each word into the blank one by one, looking for the words that seem to fit. This strategy backfires as you go along, because it will clutter your brain. Thinking to yourself, "His laconic style of speaking," "His erudite style of speaking," "His flowery style of speaking," and "His baroque style of speaking," does not tell you anything, because each of the words grammatically fits into the sentence and thus will not "sound" wrong. If you do this, soon ALL words will start to sound the same, which is a terrible state of mind for a verbal reasoning test. **Do not do this.**

The best way to find the right answers for these sentence completion problems is to try to understand the meaning of the sentence **BEFORE** you start reading the answer choices. These sentences will **ALWAYS** include enough of a context for you to understand what type of word should go into the blank. From there, you can move to the answer choices with an idea of what you want to find. Take our example sentence:

His ---- style of speaking became a problem when others found him terse and rude.

What style of speaking does this guy have? One that others may find terse and rude. Note that it is not an outright rude way of speaking; it's just one that some people can find rude. "Terse" means short and abrupt, so he does not seem rude for making long arrogant speeches, because he's coming across as rude by speaking in a short, abrupt way. Now that we understand what the sentence is saying, we can look to the answer choices to find the two words that describe this style of speaking. You can eliminate the words that do not mean terse or abrupt.

Remember: when you are going through the answer choices, **DO NOT** eliminate a word just because you do not know the definition. If you are able to reasonably eliminate the words that you do know, you should be absolutely comfortable picking a word you don't know. It is normal to not know every word, so don't dwell on it.

Laconic and *Succinct* are the two words that can mean terse or concise. These words make sense in the sentence, and create two sentences with the same meaning. *Erudite* means scholarly or knowledgeable, and *droll* means sarcastic, neither of which fits the sentence or has a synonym among the other answer choices.

These questions are not testing your vocabulary so much as they are testing your ability to understand the way words in a sentence function to create meaning. Having a strong vocabulary helps, but more important is whether you notice the relationships between words. Does a sentence invoke opposites? Make comparisons? Describe things which are *dependent upon* or *exclusive of* one another? Consider this example:

Over time it became clear that the only ------- the business's success was the commitment of its founder, who often shirked responsibility.
  a) Strategy for
  b) Boundary of
  c) Impediment to
  d) Pillar of
  e) Barrier to
  f) Force behind

This sentence and its answer choices are not full of big words. The trick to answering this question correctly is to understand the relationship in the sentence. How does the founder's commitment affect the success of the business? The founder shirks responsibility – he is not very committed. This is likely bad for the business's success, so the words that could fit the blank need to reflect that. When looking through the options, you should be looking for something that means "problem for" or "bad thing for" or something similarly negative.

Scanning through the answer choices reveals that c) and e) are the closest to reflecting this negative relationship between the flaky founder and the business's success.

A note on a bad strategy you need to avoid: For questions like this, it becomes tempting to create all kinds of wishy-washy backstories to make an answer choice fit the sentence. For the sentence above, you might have thought to yourself, "Hmmm…maybe the founder is a terrible manager, so it's actually good that he's shirking responsibility! That way his competent junior assistant can take the reins of this business and turn it into a success!" Please refrain from inserting an imagined backstory into the GRE Sentence Equivalence questions. Leave your active imagination behind (after you've written your essays). The answer to a Sentence Equivalence question will always be the most obvious, direct choice. If you find yourself mentally inserting caveats and phrases to explain a new meaning, *you are on the wrong track*. Save your imagination for grad school.

PRACTICE DRILL: SENTENCE EQUIVALENCE

Below are five practice questions. Answer these questions trying out this approach: read the sentence, think about what it is saying and what type of word should go into the blank, and then select the two answer choices which best fit this meaning. Afterwards, check your answers and read the explanations for any questions that you answered incorrectly. Actually, read the explanations for all of the questions; they will walk you through the thought process that most often leads to the correct answer.

1. The explorer was lucky that her fever was -----; for three days it had been much less severe than it had been previously.
   a) Persistent
   b) Recurrent
   c) Remittent
   d) Abating
   e) Exacerbated
   f) Surging

2. We often use the landmarks in our lives to ---- the principles towards which we are working and the things that are most important to us, such as when we set goals for a new year.
   a) Evince
   b) Undermine
   c) Obscure
   d) Accomplish
   e) Declare
   f) Marshal

3. Elliot spent little money on the gift, but he had selected it after careful listening and consideration; what it lacked in grandeur it made up for in -----.
   a) Simplicity
   b) Thought
   c) Austerity
   d) Sympathy
   e) Solicitude
   f) Propriety

4. It is important to think ---- when learning about a new place because the culture, the history, the geography, and the politics all interact to enable true understanding.
   a) Discordantly
   b) Discretely
   c) Comprehensively
   d) Critically
   e) Authentically
   f) Holistically

5. Astronomers in the 15th century were not using the precise instruments we have today; rather, they accurately ----- the distances between planetary bodies using observations and what they understood about physics on Earth.

   a) Deduced
   b) Guessed
   c) Enumerated
   d) Measured
   e) Calculated
   f) Generalized

PRACTICE DRILL: SENTENCE EQUIVALENCE – ANSWERS

1. c) and d).

From reading the sentence, you should have determined that the correct answers would mean something like "getting better" or "going away." She is lucky, and the fever is now less severe than it was before. *Persistent* and *recurrent* both indicate that the fever is staying at the same level of strength. *Exacerbated* and *surging* both indicate that the fever is getting worse. This leaves you with *remittent*, which means temporarily better, and *abating*, which means lessening or going away.

2. a) and e).

We're looking for a verb here. What are we doing when we make New Year's resolutions? We're saying what's important to us and what our values are. We want something like "say" or "state" or "decide." *Undermine* and *obscure* can both be eliminated; those words are almost opposite of what we want. *Marshal* our principals does not really make sense in this context. *Accomplish* is tempting, but does it really fit the example? Do we use New Year's to accomplish our goals, or to state them? The answers here are *declare* and *evince*. Even if you don't know what evince means (demonstrate, make clear, manifest), you can select it by eliminating the answers that do not match your initial understanding of the sentence.

3. b) and e).

We know that Elliot's gift is not expensive, but it's a good gift because he considered it carefully. The word that goes into the blank should describe this quality. Our first instinct is "thoughtfulness" or something like that. Examining the answer choices, we find *thought*, which is spot on. *Simplicity* and *austerity* can both describe something that is inexpensive, but we don't know that the gift was simple. Those words don't mean considerate. *Sympathy* and *propriety* don't hit the mark: propriety might mean appropriate to the person who received the gift, which would make sense since Elliot chose it so carefully, but the word means "proper," which isn't right. So, we go with *solicitude*, which means consideration, care, and kindness.

4. c) and f).

"Because" is a key word here. It is important to think in a certain way **because** all of these different things interact to create understanding. We are looking for a way of thinking that is important when there are a lot of different factors to consider. *Discordantly* and *discretely* both imply breaking things up and thinking about them separately – the opposite of what we want. *Critically* is always a good way to think, but it's not really a good fit with the idea of the sentence. The same is true with *authentically*. This leaves us with *holistically* and *comprehensively* – both words which mean that you are giving consideration to all of the parts of a whole.

5. **a) and e).**
    "Were not" and "rather" are key words in this sentence that signify that you'll be looking for the opposite of something stated. The ancient astronomers were NOT using precise instruments to measure a distance. However, we know that they were accurate in understanding the distances between planetary bodies using these imprecise tools. What is the opposite of measuring, but is still accurate? We're looking for a verb that means "extrapolate" or "determine" or something else you do using secondhand information to reach an accurate conclusion. *Deduced* and *calculated* give us exactly that. *Measured* and *enumerated* indicate that they are using precise instruments, which we know that they are not. *Guessed* and *generalized* indicate that they were not accurate, and we know that they were.

How did you do? If these questions troubled you, try slowing down. It's better to get three questions correct and then guess on the last two than to rush through and miss all five because you are not reading carefully.

Remember, on Sentence Equivalence questions:

- Understand the meaning of the sentence BEFORE looking at the answer choices.

- Do not be afraid to pick a word you do not know if you can eliminate the other choices.

- Pay attention to the relationships given in the sentence.

- Don't select two answers just because they are synonyms; look for words that fit your understanding of the sentence.

There are more questions like these for you to practice in the "Test Your Knowledge: Verbal Reasoning" section of this guide (page 103). If you want even more practice with Sentence Equivalence, you can also check the Resources chapter on page 173.

TEXT COMPLETION

Text Completion questions are similar to Sentence Equivalence questions. You are given a short text passage, between one and five sentences, that has one or more blanks. Each blank has its own answer choices, and you choose **ONE** answer for each blank. You get the question right by correctly selecting the answer for each blank. If a passage has three blanks and you only nail two of them, you get no credit for that question, so make sure that you carefully answer each blank in a passage. The nice thing about these is that the more blanks a passage has, the fewer answer choices are given for each blank. You might only have to select the right answer out of three choices for a given blank. The less than nice thing is that these questions can be long, so be kind to yourself and stick to your strategy.

Let's examine a Text Completion question:

Library cataloguing systems have always been important in (i)------ vast collections of knowledge; however, as information is increasingly (ii)------, methods of organizing it are changing. Information scientists are now exploring ways of archiving web sites and social media conversations in order to (iii)------ these relevant documents for the understanding of future generations.

Blank (i)	Blank (ii)	Blank (iii)
a) distilling	d) digitized	g) create
b) systematizing	e) proliferated	h) preserve
c) acquiring	f) subjective	i) interpret

How do we tackle this long question? As with Sentence Equivalence problems discussed in the previous section, the first step is to **READ THE ENTIRE TEXT**. It is tempting to jump down to the Blank (i) answer choices as soon as you come across Blank (i), but this is not a good idea. The meaning of the first sentence or phrase will almost always become clearer after you've read a bit further. You do not have to answer the blanks in order either: you can select your answers in any order, and then submit them once you're done with all three blanks.

Reading the passage without filling in the blanks yields some understanding: we're talking about the organization of information, which is becoming increasingly electronic (i.e., web sites and social media conversations). Note that those clues in the second sentence illuminate some of what is going on in the first sentence. Armed with that information, you can now look to the answer choices for each blank. Blank (ii) seems easiest: it's clear that the information has become more digitized, because we're talking about web sites in the next sentence. The answer to Blank (ii) is **d)**, digitized.

You can treat the other blanks the way you would approach a Sentence Equivalence problem. What type of word do you think should go in Blank (i)? We are talking about cataloguing and organizing information in the text; the correct answer is **b)**, systematizing. For Blank (iii), the text is describing what the purpose of archiving information is for the understanding of a future generation. An archive serves to preserve information; this is answer choice **h)**.

Nowhere in the text is *interpretation* or *creation* of information mentioned – this is all about libraries, cataloguing, archiving, and preserving digital information.

If you try to answer each blank as you go along reading the passage, it would be very easy to flub these questions. You need to understand the full context before you answer; **CONTEXT** is your new best friend for Text Completion questions.

Let's look at another text completion problem, this one shorter:

Even though the latest tests had (i)----- an outbreak as a possibility, the (ii)----- of an epidemic continued to frighten the research team.

Blank (i)	Blank (ii)
a) Confirmed	d) Specter
b) Eliminated	e) Likelihood
c) Explored	f) Absurdity

This Text Completion problem is simple, but not necessarily easy. Remember: the most important thing is to understand the relationships between the words in the sentence to understand the underlying meaning. "Even though" is one of those key phrases, signifying that while one thing is happening, something else is happening that is contradictory to the first thing. Think about this sentence: "Even though I had no money, I still went out with my friends." I had no money, so I should NOT have gone out. But that "even though" lets you know that I did the opposite of what the first phrase would indicate.

Now, this Text Completion is like a two-part puzzle; you can't really fill in one blank and then move on to the next. You have to understand the sentence enough to simultaneously fill both blanks in a way that makes sense. This is VERY common to this question type, and you need to be comfortable and confident answering this type of question. Almost any combination of choices for the two blanks makes a sentence that *kind of* makes sense, but only one *really* makes sense, and it's our job to find it.

Okay: the research team did some tests regarding the possibility of an outbreak of some disease, and even though the test results said something the team is still frightened about this outbreak. THIS is the meaning of the sentence, and distilling these blank-riddled texts into a phrase like this one is a skill you can practice.

Knowing that this is the meaning of the sentence, what kind of words should we expect for the two blanks? The research team is still scared even after those test results, so the test probably *ruled out* the possibility of an outbreak, which should have allayed the fear of the team. For the second blank, our guess would be something like "possibility" or "threat:" something that indicates that the team was scared in the first place. Going to the answer choices, it is clear that **b)** and **d)** are the right choices: "eliminated" is very close to "ruled out," and "specter" is pretty close to "threat."

These problems build on your Sentence Equivalence skills, but sometimes require that extra cognitive step it takes to hold the whole meaning of the sentence in your head with multiple blanks. Just remember that these questions are constructed to be solved, so *there is a right answer, and you have all the information you need to find it.* You just need to read – and think – carefully.

PRACTICE DRILL: TEXT COMPLETION

Try these sample questions, and then read the explanations for them to see how you're doing in building this skill. Each explanation will present a different strategy or tool that can help you as you practice this type of question.

1. Jeff was unconditionally (i)----- about his idea; try as we might, we could not (ii)----- him.

Blank (i)	Blank (ii)
a) Ambivalent	g) Dissuade
b) Adamant	h) Convince
c) Pragmatic	i) Persuade

2. It took a good deal of trial and error for the city's bus schedule to be perfected; in the early days of the service, there were ------ nearly every week.

Problems

a) Adjustments
b) Collisions
c) Vagaries
d) Protests
e) Exigencies

3. Insects cause a serious annual monetary loss to the people of the United States. Grain fields are (i)------; orchards and gardens are destroyed or seriously (ii)-----; forests are made waste places. In scores of other ways these little pests are (iii)----- this tremendous tax.

Blank (i)	Blank (ii)	Blank (iii)
a) Reaped	d) Mutilated	g) Remunerating
b) Inaugurated	e) Demolished	h) Exacting
c) Devastated	f) Razed	i) Ruining

4. In psychology, the study of heuristics explores mental shortcuts people develop based on their experiences over time. We (i)----- heuristics to save time and energy when making decisions about something for which we have (ii)----- ideas and emotions based on past experience or learned information. However, this strategy can (iii)----- when it leads to the formation of misleading biases.

faulty

Blank (i)	Blank (ii)	Blank (iii)
a) Employ	d) Palty	g) Backfire
b) Contend with	e) Skewed	h) Overwhelm
c) Discount	f) Preconceived	i) Bode well

24

5. The student deplored those who opted to study the ----- volume of literature; she felt that one could never understand the classics by only reading excerpted chapters out of the context of the original novels.

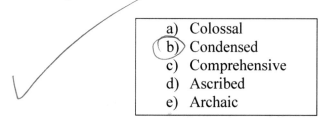

a) Colossal
b) Condensed
c) Comprehensive
d) Ascribed
e) Archaic

PRACTICE DRILL: TEXT COMPLETION – ANSWERS

1. b) and g)
From the sentence, we know that Jeff has an idea and that we are trying really hard but failing to do something about it. This is one of those two-blank problems for which you have to answer both blanks at once for the sentence to make sense. The word "unconditionally" is a good clue here: we know that Jeff is extreme about his idea, so he's either totally for it or totally against it. If he's totally for it, then we're trying to talk him out of it and failing. If he's totally against his idea (which would be weird, but possible), then we're trying to talk him into it and failing. Only one of these can be right, so let's look at the answer choices and see which one we find. For Blank (i), we can immediately eliminate *pragmatic* (practical) and *ambivalent* (undecided), because they do not fit this narrative; Jeff has to be either unconditionally for or against this idea of his. This leaves us with *adamant*: Jeff is adamant about his idea, and he's not going to budge. That means we must be trying to talk him out of it, and failing. For Blank (ii), "talk him out of" is closest to "dissuade," so **g)** is correct. Note that for Blank (ii), it would be easy to mistakenly pick *convince* or *persuade* if you haven't thought through the problem.

Strategy note: for questions where you can only pick one answer per blank, like the Text Completion, you can eliminate answer choices which are synonyms because they cannot both be correct. *Convince* and *persuade* would mean the same thing in this sentence. If they can't both be right, then neither can be right. You won't see this often, but it is good to check for.

2. a)
We know from reading the sentence that in the early days of the bus service the schedule was not perfect, and there was a lot of trial and error being done. There are two logical ways to fill in the blank: in the early days there could have been delays or other problems every week, or there could have been changes every week as the city tried to perfect the schedule. Looking at the choices, *adjustment* makes the most sense with this idea. *Collisions* are indeed bad things that could result from a terrible bus schedule, but that's pretty dramatic, and the sentence does not give any context to indicate that this is happening. Likewise with *protests*: a bad bus schedule could result in protests, but there would need to be something else in the sentence indicating this for it to be a good option. For example, if the sentence said something about the citizens being fed up with the bus system, then *protests* might fit. *Vagaries* and *exigencies* are big words that don't fit the

25

sentence, but that doesn't matter because *adjustments* works so perfectly that you don't have to worry about the other choices (*exigencies* are emergencies, and *vagaries* are whims or impulses).

3. **c), d), and h)**
There is a lot of context in this sentence, so it is easy to understand the general meaning without filling in the blanks: insects are causing a lot of damage to plants in the United States. Because we understand the whole sentence pretty well, we can look at each phrase to fill in the blanks. For Blank (i), we know it will be a negative word, like "harmed" or "ruined" because this immediately follows the statement that insects cause monetary loss, without any kind of qualifier such as "however" or "except." *Devastated* is the only word in the Blank (i) answer choices which fits this meaning. Blank (ii) is a little more nuanced. The phrase says "orchards and gardens are destroyed or seriously ----." The word in this blank cannot be a synonym for destroyed, like "ruined" or "devastated," because the phrase says that they are destroyed OR something else. When "or" is used, the words being related cannot by synonyms.

For example, you would not say "I'm going to be excited OR enthusiastic when that new album comes out on Friday." So, we need a word for Blank (ii) that is negative, but is not a synonym for destroyed. *Mutilated* is the only answer choice that fits this. Something can be mutilated without being totally destroyed, because it means seriously injured or damaged. The other words, *razed* and *demolished*, are synonyms for "destroyed." The last sentence describes all this damage as a "tremendous tax." What are the insects doing when they inflict all this damage? They are the ones taking this "tax." For Blank (iii), *exacting* is the only answer choice that fits the meaning of the insects taking this tax. *Remunerating* means that they are paying it, and *ruining* doesn't really fit the meaning of this sentence, but it does trickily go along with the other answer choices, so some might be tempted to choose it.

4. **a), f), and g)**
This one is harder to decode at first glance, because the test introduces terminology likely unfamiliar to you, unless you studied it in college. Questions that draw from more specific wells of knowledge are common on the GRE. Remember, they are giving you everything you need to know to answer the question, regardless of whether you've heard of "heuristics" before. Let's get a general idea of the meaning of the passage: heuristics are mental shortcuts that people develop over time. People make decisions based on their past experiences, which saves time, but sometimes this can lead to the formation of biases.

Okay, now that we understand the text, let's examine Blank (i). Heuristics are shortcuts we develop over time; this suggests that they are positive and useful. We could say that we "use" them to make decisions. Answer choice **a)**, *employ*, is a synonym for "use" and is the correct answer. Choices **b)** and **c)** both indicate that heuristics are negative, and this part of the text does not describe them in that way. Blank (ii) describes when we use heuristics. The first sentence explains that we develop them based on our past experiences over time, so it makes sense that we use them when we are dealing with something that we already have experience with and ideas about. Choice **f)**, *preconceived*, is the same as "already have."

Again, the other two answer choices are negative in tone. ETS will use this trick: the choices are negative in tone because the end of the text shifts to a negative tone. However, when filling in the blanks at the beginning of the text, we should match the tone used there. In this text, the beginning is neutral, or even positive, in tone. Now we come to the last sentence. The tone shift to negative is indicated by "however," and then the text describes that heuristics can lead to unhelpful biases. What is the strategy doing when it misleads a person rather than helping them to make the right decisions? We should look for something that means "doesn't work." Answer choice **g)**, *backfires*, fits this meaning exactly.

5. **b)**

This sentence is a good example of why it's not a good idea to read each word back into the blank to check how it sounds. Each of the answer choices fits well in the blank, and each could sensibly fit the situation. However, the best word is *condensed* because it best fits with the additional information given in the sentence: this student deplores the literature volume because it only presents some chapters of the classics rather than the full novels. It is shortened, edited, *condensed*. There is no similar argument to support choosing any of the other words.

Just remember: exposure to these types of questions gives you a HUGE leg up in performing well on test day. There are more questions in the Verbal Reasoning practice material in the back of this guide.

READING COMPREHENSION

Many people find this section of the test to be the hardest, because they are unprepared for the types of passages they will be reading. The Verbal Reasoning Reading Comprehension passages are not narrative; they are academic. You are being tested, again, on your ability to understand the structure of an argument. Remember this as you are reading. You want to look for logic and reasoning used within the passages.

The passages tend to be short (one to three paragraphs), but they are dense and present complicated arguments. However, the questions are concrete, and the correct answer will always be supported in the text. You can ace the Reading Comprehension by reading carefully and learning how to look to the text for answers. This section will provide examples of the types of passages on the GRE and will model for you the thought processes you should use to correctly answer the questions that follow.

There are a lot of different kinds of readers who will take the GRE. Some people read very quickly, but may fail to fully understand everything they read the first time through. Others are more deliberate readers, who don't move on from a sentence until they are sure they understand it. It is best on these passages to take an approach somewhere in the middle of these tendencies: you don't want to skim the passage, because then you'll have to go back and reread entire sections when you're answering a question, which is a waste of time. However, you should not get so hung up on understanding every word that you spend too much time on a passage which might only have one or two questions asked about it. Learn your best pace in the practice sections provided in this guide, and stick to that pace if you find yourself getting bogged down or skimming when you read during the GRE.

> **Slower readers:** Remember that every question is worth the same amount of points, so if you find yourself getting bogged down on one question or if a passage looks immediately daunting to you, you can always skip that question or mark that passage to return to it after you've done the other ones.

> **Skimmers:** Remember that there is no point in answering every question if you've answered half of them wrong. Try to focus carefully on the passage in front of you, even if it takes a little extra time, to make sure that you're getting all the points that you can.

ETS gets a bit creative with the question format on the Reading Comprehension sections. Some questions will ask you to select all answer choices that apply, and other questions may ask you to just highlight a particular sentence on the screen that serves a given function in the passage. Make sure you **read the directions for *each question* carefully** to ensure that you answer in the correct way.

Strategy Tip for Passages with One Question versus Passages with More:
Across the top of the screen displaying a passage will be a note on how many questions are based on that passage. If there's only one question associated with a passage, you're looking at it: the text will display on the left of the screen and the question will display on the right.

In these cases, go ahead and read the question first so you'll know what to look for when you read the passage. HOWEVER, if you see that a passage has more than one question associated with it, don't bother reading the questions first. You'll need to carefully read the passage first, knowing that you'll have to think critically about the whole thing.

PRACTICE DRILL: READING COMPREHENSION

The collapse of the financial arbitrage firm Long-Term Capital Management (LTCM) in 1998 is explained by a host of different factors: its investments were based on a high level of leverage, for example, and it was significantly impacted by Russia's default on the ruble. However, sociologist Donald MacKenzie maintains that the main factor in LTCM's demise was that, like all arbitrage firms, it was subjected to the sociological phenomena of the arbitrage community; namely, imitation. Arbitrageurs, who are generally known to one another as members of a specific subset of the financial society, use decision-making strategies based not only on mathematical models or pure textbook reason, but also based upon their feelings and gut reactions toward the financial market and on the actions of their peers. This imitation strategy leads to an overlapping "superportfolio" among the firms, which creates an inherent instability.

The public opinion of the partners of the firm in 1998 was that it had acted cavalierly with borrowed capital. However, in actuality the firm's strategy was exceedingly conservative, with a diversified portfolio, overestimated risks, and carefully hedged investments. The firm even tested tactics for dealing with financial emergencies such as the collapse of the European Monetary Union. Before the 1998 crisis, those of LTCM were never accused of recklessness. Nor were they, as is sometimes explained, overly reliant on mathematical models. The statistical hubris explanation falters under MacKenzie's evidence that John Meriwether and the others who ran the firm made their investment decisions based more upon their intricate understandings of the arbitrage market rather than upon the pure results of mathematical analyses. The financial instability that was created was not the result of the decision-making of one firm; but rather, the collective patterns of decision-making of all of the arbitrage firms at the time.

Directions: Select One Answer Choice

1. The author includes the information presented in the second paragraph of this text primarily to:
   a) Explain that recklessness with borrowed capital is not profitable.
   b) Explore the factors ultimately responsible for the demise of the arbitrage firm Long-Term Capital Management.
   c) Explain the use of statistical models in calculating financial risks.
   d) Present and dismiss several theories of the collapse of Long-Term Capital Management.
   e) Argue that a sociological framework can be used to assess the collapse of a financial firm.

2. Which of the following assertions could undermine Mackenzie's reasoning as outlined in the passage?
   a) The European Monetary Union was close to collapse in 1998.
   b) Some arbitrage firms steered clear of the practice of superportfolios.
   c) Arbitrageurs rarely communicate with one another or get information from the same source.
   d) Mathematical models used in finance in the 1990s were highly reliable.
   e) What arbitrageurs consider their "gut instinct" is often a subconscious conclusion drawn from a number of information sources.

Directions: Select All Answer Choices That Are Correct

3. According to the passage, which of the following statements about Long-Term Capital Management was true before its collapse?
   a) The partners of the firm employed the imitation strategy.
   b) The investing strategies of the firm were carefully selected and made use of mathematical models.
   c) The public held a clear understanding regarding the actions of the firm.
   d) The firm resisted building a "superportfolio" because of the inherent riskiness of that strategy.
   e) The partners of the firm were accused of acting recklessly and cavalierly with their investments.

Directions: Select One Answer Choice

4. In the argument given in this passage, the two highlighted sentences serve what functions?
   a) The first presents an argument against the thesis of the passage, and the second explains why that argument is false.
   b) The first supports the author's assertion that arbitrageurs act within a community, and the second gives further evidence for the conclusion drawn in this paragraph.
   c) The first presents a counter-argument to the central idea of the passage, and the second presents another counter-argument.
   d) The first dismisses a misconception concerning the passage's subject, and the second gives further support to the author's central argument.
   e) The first states an argument against the central idea of the passage, and the second refutes another counter-argument stated elsewhere in the paragraph.

PRACTICE DRILL: READING COMPREHENSION – ANSWERS

Remember, the correct answers can always be supported in the text. It's important to note every word in the question and how it may change the meaning of the question. Let's look at the answers, along with the strategies used to get them. The sections below include general strategy tips for all Verbal Reasoning questions, so you should read all of them even if you did not find a particular question difficult.

Question 1

This question is asking you to evaluate the function of the second paragraph in the context of the passage overall. This is a common type of question, because the GRE emphasizes verbal organization and the flow of logic. You see this in Verbal Reasoning questions and in the evaluation of the Analytical Writing essays. As you read the Verbal passages, you should read with an eye to **organization and logic**. What are the author's points? What is the overarching goal of the piece? How does each sentence and paragraph serve to support the author's argument or the information given? You will never see an open-ended or fictional piece. The source materials are academic, and the passages build arguments.

This passage is about the collapse of a financial investment firm, LCTM, and more specifically about one theory of its collapse. Notice the structure of a passage as you read it: by the second sentence, we are given the main thesis of the piece. The first paragraph outlines this argument, and the second paragraph presents alternate explanations and briefly debunks them in favor of the thesis argument. This is something you should see as you read through the passage for the first time. If you need to, you can always take brief notes on your scratch paper as you read to mark the logical flow of the passage. So, we understand what the question is asking, and we should have a general idea of what the right answer will be. It's time to evaluate the answer choices.

Sometimes the Verbal Reasoning reading comprehension questions are less about finding the right answer and more about getting rid of all the wrong answers. Answer choices can be wrong for several reasons:

- They are inaccurate given the information presented in the passage.

- They are true statements with regard to the passage, but they do not answer the question asked.

- They are true and relevant to the question, but they are incomplete answers and another answer choice gives a more complete answer.

Keep these in mind when evaluating an answer choice:

- Is it *true with regard to the passage*?

- Is it *answering the question asked*?

- Is it the *best answer choice given*?

Also, remember that some questions allow you to select more than one answer choice. You should read the directions to know this going in, but if you find yourself stuck between two answers that seem true, you can **check the directions** to see if they can both be selected.

Let's apply these criteria to the answer choices given for the first question. Does the author include the information in paragraph two primarily to:

a) *Explain that recklessness with borrowed capital is not profitable*? Is this statement true with regard to the passage? Does the author explain that recklessness is not profitable? No. The author states that LTCM was not reckless, despite public opinion. The profitability of recklessness is never mentioned. This statement is wrong.

b) *Explore the factors ultimately responsible for the demise of the arbitrage firm Long-Term Capital Management*? Is this statement true with regard to the passage? Well, the paragraph does examine different possible factors, but it dismisses them as those not ultimately responsible for the firm's demise. This one is half-true.

c) *Explain the use of statistical models in calculating financial risks*? Is this statement true with regard to the passage? Yes, the author does explain how the firm used statistical models: the partners did have mathematical analyses, but used them in tandem with other sources of information. Does this statement answer the question directly? No, the paragraph is not **primarily** about this at all; the use of statistical models is only one small part of the paragraph. This is enough to reject this answer choice.

d) *Present and dismiss several theories of the collapse of Long-Term Capital Management*? Is this statement true with regard to the passage? Yes. We already noted that the second paragraph presents alternative theories of the firm's collapse: the recklessness theory and the reliance on mathematical models theory. The author then gives a brief argument as to why each is wrong. Therefore, the entire statement is true with regard to the passage. Is this the best answer choice? So far: yes. Let's look at **e)** to be sure.

e) *Argue that a sociological framework can be used to assess the collapse of a financial firm?* Is this statement true with regard to the passage? Well, the entire passage is about using a sociological framework to understand the collapse of LTCM, so in that sense it is true. However, is this the purpose of the second paragraph specifically? No, the paragraph is less about using sociology than it is about why the other interpretations of the firm's collapse are wrong. Is this the best answer choice? No, **d)** is still the best choice.

Question 2
This question gives you a list of facts that are not presented in the passage and asks you to evaluate how they would affect MacKenzie's argument. This is also a common reading comprehension question type on the GRE. You have to not only understand what is presented in the passage, but also infer how other information would affect the passage's argument. Some passages present more than one argument, so you should be sure that you are clear on which one you are being asked to consider. For this passage, MacKenzie (the sociologist) is the only one whose argument is presented. So, before you look at the answer choices, make sure you're clear on what his argument is. Let's try to sum up the argument of the passage in a sentence: The firm Long-Term Capital Management collapsed primarily because it was part of a financial community weakened by everyone making the same investment decisions.

Okay, now we can look at the answer choices. We are looking for the statement that, if true, would undermine this argument. Remember that the right answers can always be supported by the text.

a) *The European Monetary Union was close to collapse in 1998.* What does the passage say about the European Monetary Union? It is mentioned in the second paragraph; LTCM had strategies in place for dealing with the potential collapse of the Union. So, does saying that the Union was close to collapse undermine the argument? No, the argument says that LTCM acted in cautious ways to avoid these kinds of financial threats.

b) *Some arbitrage firms steered clear of the practice of superportfolios.* What does the passage say about superportfolios? It defines the term as the overarching investment pattern created when a lot of arbitrage firms make similar investment decisions. Would the existence of some firms that avoided this practice undermine the overall argument of the passage? Maybe it would weaken the argument a little, because the idea of a superportfolio requires firms to be acting in the same way, but there's no clear reason for why some firms not participating would undermine the argument of the passage. Let's see if there's a better answer.

34

c) *Arbitrageurs rarely communicate with one another or get information from the same source.* What does the passage say about how arbitrageurs communicate and where they get information? The first paragraph explains that they are generally known to one another and often make decisions based on their similar instincts and on what others in the community are doing. The passage also explains that this behavior is what creates the superportfolio, which led to the firm's collapse. This answer choice directly contradicts this, and does so for arbitrageurs in general, not just some of them as in answer choice **b)**. This statement would clearly undermine the thesis of the passage.

d) *Mathematical models used in finance in the 1990s were highly reliable.* What does the passage say about mathematical models? It says that some people suggested that the collapse of LTCM was due to a reliance on them, but that in actuality the firm did not solely rely on mathematical analysis of markets. If these models were reliable, would that change the strength of the passage's argument? Maybe one could argue that the firm's downfall was because they did not solely rely on the mathematical models, but this is (tangential) to the superportfolio theory. It would weaken the argument, but not directly undermine it. *Slightly Connected*

e) *What arbitrageurs consider their "gut instinct" is often a subconscious conclusion drawn from a number of information sources.* What does the passage say about arbitrageurs' gut instincts? In the first paragraph, it is stated that arbitrageurs made decisions partially based on their gut reactions to the markets and to other firms' decisions. The statement in this answer choice elaborates more on how those reactions form, but it doesn't contradict anything stated in the passage.

Out of these answer choices, the one that best undermines MacKenzie's argument is answer choice **c)**. Did you notice the pattern in how we evaluated each answer choice? The first step in these types of questions is always to go back to the text to see what the passage says about the topic mentioned. The right answer choice can always be supported by something in the passage. When a question gives you new pieces of information and asks you to evaluate them within the context of the passage, you should always refer to the text this way.

Question 3
A "select all that apply" question! When answering these questions, remember:

- Sometimes only one option is right.

- *At least* one option is right, so you must select at least one to answer the question.

- An answer choice should be entirely true before you select it.

- *All* of the answer choices can potentially be correct; you can select them all.

The nice thing about these questions is that you don't have to decide between answer choices. The hard thing is that you have to carefully evaluate each choice; you can't skim over the rest once you've found one that is right. (Not that you should do that anyway, since there can always be a better answer choice.)

The question asks which of the following statements was true about LCTM before its collapse. Take note of the whole question: you're looking for statements that were true *before* the firm's collapse. The passage discusses the firm from the perspective of looking back after the collapse, so you have to be careful not to conflate the public theories and opinions from after the collapse with the truth about the firm before that point. Okay, to answer this question, we need to evaluate each answer choice on its own merits:

a) *The partners of the firm employed the imitation strategy.* Is this true? Yes, the passage gives evidence that the partners, like most arbitrageurs, took cues from others in the field. This is what created the superportfolio. We should select this choice.

b) *The investing strategies of the firm were carefully selected and made use of mathematical models.* Is this true? Yes, the passage states that the firm used conservative and carefully hedged investment strategies. It also states that they did not overly rely on mathematical models, but does not imply that those models weren't used at all. We should also select this choice.

c) *The public held a clear understanding regarding the actions of the firm.* Is this true? According to the passage, after the collapse the public felt that the firm's partners had acted cavalierly with their capital. The passage shows this not to be true, so we can assume that the public did not have a clear understanding of the firm's actions at any time. We should not select this choice.

d) *The firm resisted building a "superportfolio" because of the inherent riskiness of that strategy.* Is this true? According to the passage, LCTM's participation in the superportfolio culture is what led to its collapse. There is no evidence that LCTM resisted this, so we should not select this choice.

e) *The partners of the firm were accused of acting recklessly and cavalierly with their investments.* Is this true? We know that it was true after the firm's collapse. Is there any evidence that the public considered the firm reckless before the collapse? The passage states that "before the 1998 crisis, those of LTCM were never accused of recklessness." We should not select this choice.

The correct answer choices are **a)** and **b)**. Notice that we look for specific evidence in the text to back up each choice.

Question 4

Notice that the directions tell us to go back to selecting only one answer choice. How does this affect how we answer? We have to ask not only if each answer choice is true, but if it is the *best* answer choice. This question solves the mystery of why two sentences in the passage are highlighted: so that we can evaluate the functions that those sentences serve!

This question asks you about the purposes of the two sentences, and the answer choices are given as a series of assumptions about the first sentence and then the second. These kinds of questions are common on the reading comprehension section of the GRE – you may be asked to evaluate the functions of two sentences, or two paragraphs, or two facts, or two points of view. The trick is that BOTH parts of the answer choice must be correct for you to select it. An answer choice might perfectly describe the function of Sentence 1, and then falter when it comes to Sentence 2. The *best* answer choice will accurately describe BOTH things you are being asked to evaluate. In some ways this makes eliminating bad answer choices easier, but it can lead you to be tempted by an answer choice that is only halfway correct, so read carefully. Here are the sentences we're evaluating for this question:

Sentence 1: The public opinion of the partners of the firm in 1998 was that it had acted cavalierly with borrowed capital.

Sentence 2: The statistical hubris explanation falters under MacKenzie's evidence that John Meriwether and the others who ran the firm made their investment decisions based more upon their intricate understandings of the arbitrage market rather than upon the pure results of mathematical analyses.

Remember, you should be looking at these in the context of the passage. Luckily, that's easy on the GRE where you will have a split-screen with the entire passage presented to you at all times.

Now, let's look at the choices for this question:

a) *The first presents an argument against the thesis of the passage, and the second explains why that argument is false.* Is this true? Let's evaluate that separately for each sentence. Sentence 1: does this present an argument against the thesis of the passage? What is the thesis of the passage? That the main factor in the collapse of LTCM was the sociological phenomenon of imitation. Sentence 1 does give an alternate explanation: that the firm was cavalier. This statement is true regarding Sentence 1. What about Sentence 2? Does it explain why the argument presented in Sentence 1 is false? No, it is explaining why the argument that the firm was overly reliant on mathematical models is false. It does not refute Sentence 1. Eliminate Choice **a)**!

b) *The first supports the author's assertion that arbitrageurs act within a community, and the second gives further evidence for the conclusion drawn in this paragraph.* Is this true? Does Sentence 1 support the author's assertion about arbitrageurs working in a community? No, it has nothing to do with that. We can eliminate Choice **b)**!

c) *The first presents a counter-argument to the central idea of the passage, and the second presents another counter-argument.* Is this true? Does Sentence 1 present a counter-argument to the passage's thesis? Yes, we said that above when evaluating Choice **a)**. Okay, does Sentence 2 present another counter-argument? No, Sentence 2 is refuting a counter-argument that was presented earlier in the paragraph. We can eliminate Choice **c)**!

d) *The first dismisses a misconception concerning the passage's subject, and the second gives further support to the author's central argument.* Is this true? Does Sentence 1 dismiss a misconception concerning the subject of the passage? It addresses a misconception held by the public, but doesn't dismisses it. Let's suspend judgment on Sentence 1 and look at Sentence 2. Does Sentence 2 give further support to the author's central argument? Yes, it is clarifying how those in the firm made their decisions, which contributes to the imitation theory. Choice **d)** is not as wrong as the others, but it's not quite right. Let's check Choice **e)**.

e) *The first states an argument against the central idea of the passage, and the second refutes another counter-argument stated elsewhere in the paragraph.* Is this true? Let's look at Sentence 1: yes, we've said above that it presents a counter-argument to the thesis of the passage. That counter-argument is that LCTM acted cavalierly with capital, as understood by the public. What about Sentence 2? Yes, we said while evaluating choice C that it is repudiating a counter-argument presented previously in the paragraph. We can select Choice **e)**, which is the right answer.

These long reading comprehension passages can be grueling. Fortunately, some of the reading passages on the GRE are much shorter. The questions are still abstruse, but at least we don't have think about the same topic for more than a few minutes. Let's try one of these shorter passages. This one has two questions:

> The constructivist theory of cognitive development focuses on an individual's attempt to organize information about the world into structures. As an adolescent learns and assimilates more information, his or her cognitive structures advance in a way that allows the understanding of complex and abstract theories and ideas. The theory makes use of a block-stage structure, in which humans must first learn to understand certain types of information before they have the ability to understand more complex information. In this way, humans "construct" their own understanding of the world using tools that they have previously developed. Constructivist psychologists believe that learning occurs when a human encounters a fact, idea, or experience that contradicts what he or she already knows. The person then attempts to reconcile the datum with extant knowledge by deepening their understanding through a process termed "equilibration."

Directions: Select All Answers That Apply

1. The constructivist theory of cognitive development would be supported by the observation of:
   a) A child giving nonsensical answers to questions about abstract concepts.
   b) An adolescent rejecting an idea because it does not fit his experience.
   c) An adult researching an idea that conflicts with her beliefs.

Directions: Select One Answer Choice

2. Another theoretical perspective regarding cognitive development is Behaviorism, which holds that knowledge and behavior are enforced by patterns in the environment and by meaningful repetition of actions. Feedback from others is integral to the learning process, according to Behaviorists. Positive feedback reinforces desirable behaviors, which is how others learn. Constructivists and Behaviorists would both agree with which of the following points?
   a) Students who encounter new ideas are learning.
   b) Practical, real-world experiences are necessary for learning.
   c) Different types of knowledge must be learned in different ways.
   d) Repetition is the most effective way to process new information.
   e) Cognitive development occurs only with outside input.

The "select all that apply" questions can be nice, because they often have only three or four answer choices rather than the standard five. The challenge is that you must carefully evaluate each answer choice regardless of whether you've already found an answer you agree with. Then, notice that the directions switch for the second question, back to the standard "select one answer."

Let's take a look at the answers.

Question 1

Our first move, before checking out the answer choices, is to make sure we understand the constructivist theory of cognitive development. Can we sum it up, based on our reading of the passage? Let's summarize: the theory that learning occurs as people assimilate new information into their structures of knowledge.

Now what are we looking for? Observations *supporting* this theory. Okay, next we evaluate the answer choices one at a time, looking for support from the passage to accept or reject a choice:

a) *A child giving nonsensical answers to questions about abstract concepts.* The passage doesn't explicitly mention children, but it does say that adolescence is when humans have enough experience in their cognitive structures to understand abstract ideas. Using the constructivist theory, would we expect a child to think abstractly? No, so this observation would support the theory. We should select it.

b) *An adolescent rejecting an idea because it does not fit his experience.* What does the passage say about accepting or rejecting ideas? It says that learning occurs when people try to understand an idea that conflicts with the ones they already hold. This choice is saying that an adolescent is observed rejecting an idea without attempting the equilibration process, so that would undermine the constructivist model rather than support it. We should *not* select this choice.

c) *An adult researching an idea that conflicts with her beliefs.* This would support what we say above; it would show a person going through the equilibration process. This supports the theoretical model, and we should select it.

The correct answers are **a) and c)**.

Question 2
This question explains another theoretical model for understanding cognitive development, and then asks us to identify the point on which proponents of the theory presented in the passage and this second theory would agree.

Do we understand the second perspective given to us in the question? Behaviorism states that learning occurs when others in the environment give feedback to our actions. Let's look at the answer choices and evaluate why each one might be right. Remember, we're looking for the statement that both a Constructivist and a Behaviorist would agree with:

    a) *Students who encounter new ideas are learning.* Does a Constructivist think this? Yes, learning is what happens when we assimilate new ideas into our existing structures of thought, according to that theory. Would a Behaviorist? Not necessarily; this doesn't say anything about whether students get feedback regarding their reaction to the new idea. We can probably eliminate this answer choice.

    b) *Practical, real-world experiences are necessary for learning.* Does a Constructivist think this? No, the passage never says this. We can eliminate this answer choice.

    c) *Different types of knowledge must be learned in different ways.* Neither theory mentions this idea. Maybe this would be a way to reconcile multiple theories of cognitive development, but that doesn't mean that the different theorists would agree on that. We can eliminate this answer choice.

    d) *Repetition is the most effective way to process new information.* Does a Constructivist agree with this? No; repetition is nothing like the equilibration process. This is a pretty accurate description of the Behaviorist theory, but the two would not agree. Eliminate this answer choice.

    e) *Cognitive development occurs only with outside input.* Does a Constructivist agree with this? Yes; new ideas and concepts must challenge existing cognitive structures for learning to occur. Would a Behaviorist agree with this? Yes; outside feedback is necessary for learning to occur. We have our answer!

Remember that even if you find what you believe to be the best answer midway through the answer choices, you should still skim the rest of them to make sure that there's not a better one. If you only have a few minutes left, don't bother, but it is usually good practice.

Okay, let's try one more quick passage. This is another short passage, and it has only one question associated with it. You can read the question before you read the passage, if you want to try that strategy. Remember, you should only read the question first if a passage has only one question associated with it. You don't want to read the passage looking for the answer to a specific question when you have to answer others as well, because you will end having to reread most of the passage.

An excerpt from the Clive Bell's seminal art history book <u>Art</u> (public domain):

> To criticize a work of art historically is to play the science-besotted fool. No more disastrous theory ever issued from the brain of a charlatan than that of evolution in art. Giotto did not creep, a grub, that Titian might flaunt, a butterfly. To praise or abuse or be interested in a work of art because it leads or does not lead to another work of art is to treat it as though it were not a work of art. The connection of one work of art with another may have everything to do with history: it has nothing to do with appreciation. As soon as we begin to consider a work as anything else than an end in itself we leave the world of art. Though the development of painting from Giotto to Titian may be interesting historically, it cannot affect the value of any particular picture: aesthetically, it is of no consequence whatever.

1. The passage asserts which of the following about the relationship between aesthetic judgments of art and historical understanding of art?
   a) Understanding the historical predecessors of a work of art allows one to make a more informed aesthetic judgment.
   b) It is more important to understand the aesthetic value of a work of art than it is to study its place in a historical tradition of artwork.
   c) To account for the historical position of a work of art while judging its aesthetic merits is anathema.
   d) The evolution of a style of art as artists learn from those who have come before them is what enables aesthetic judgments to develop.
   e) The debate over what makes something a work of art can be argued in both historical and aesthetic contexts.

Think through each answer choice and select the one you find best.

Questions relating two concepts within a passage are quite common, so it's important when you read to get a feel for the author's perspective regarding each concept the passage brings up. The reading comprehension passages on the GRE center on ideas, arguments, counter-arguments, evidence, and theories. You should become comfortable distinguishing concepts an author agrees with from those he or she brings up in order to refute.

The author of this passage states that the history of a work of art should play no part in judging the aesthetic value of that work. For this reason, you should have eliminated answers **a)** and **d)**. Choice **b)** is tricky; the author certainly seems to value aesthetics more than history, but he never explicitly states this and even says that "the connection of one work of art to another may have everything to do with history." For this reason, we can eliminate choice **b)**. Choice **e)** may be true, but it is not suggested by the author. Choice **c)** is the correct answer: he feels that it is foolish and disastrous to use historical context to criticize the aesthetics of a work of art. "Anathema" means that something is strongly denounced. Even if you were not familiar with that word, you should have arrived at Choice **c)** through eliminating the other choices.

Final Tips:

On the Reading Comprehension questions, remember:

- Read the entire question, and note any qualifying statements in the question.

- Check answers to see if they are true regarding the passage.

- Look for evidence supporting your answer choice in the passage.

- Follow the directions to ensure that you're answering in the right way.

And that is how you trounce the GRE reading comprehension passages! Practice definitely helps to make these less intimidating, so try the practice questions in the Verbal Practice chapter.

to beat severely; thrash

Chapter 2: Quantitative Reasoning

Do you remember your high school math classes? If not, you should definitely brush up on the math skills you learned in high school because those are exactly what the GRE Quantitative Reasoning sections are all about. Maybe your undergraduate degree was in Comparative Literature and you have not thought about math in years other than to divide a dinner check. Or perhaps you were a Mathematics major and you've been doing math so complicated, and abstract that you do not remember how to find the mode in a number set. More likely than not, you're somewhere in between.

In any event, it will be beneficial to read this chapter. You should also attempt the practice problems in the Quantitative Reasoning Practice chapter – the explanations and answers to these problems are very thorough.

The GRE Quantitative Reasoning section covers four basic types of math: **arithmetic, simple algebra, geometry,** and **data analysis**. It sticks close to the surface in each of those categories: no Moments of Inertia or Gaussian probabilities here!

inactivity

> **Math lovers**: Do not rely on your facility with numbers to get you through this section. These questions are tricky, and you need to be familiar with the ways they are asked to avoid answer traps. Your math aptitude will be very useful, but don't get over-confident and let it be your downfall.

> **Non math lovers**: Don't worry; the math tested in the majority of these problems is pretty basic. The real test of your reasoning ability comes with the tricks and traps the ETS employs, and you will do fine once you've reviewed the basic concepts.

Okay, let's get to it!

Structure of the Quantitative Reasoning Sections

You will have two scored Quantitative Reasoning sections, and you may have one additional experimental section that will not. Each Quantitative section will be 25 questions long, and you will have 40 minutes to answer.

You can skip around within the section to answer questions in any order you like, and all questions within a section will be worth the same number of points. Remember, there's no penalty for answering a question wrong, so you should guess on those you haven't solved before the end of your time.

You will see three different question structures within these sections:

- *Quantitative Comparison* questions, which will give you two different quantities and ask you to select whether Quantity A or Quantity B is greater, the quantities are the same, or this information cannot be determined based on what is provided.

- *Numeric Entry* questions, which do not have answer choices but instead ask you to type in the value that you have calculated to be the answer.

- *Multiple Choice* questions, which will give you a set of possible answers. Some of these will require you to select only one answer; others will direct you to select all that apply. PAY ATTENTION to the directions so that you answer these properly.

You are not allowed to bring in your own calculator for the test, but one is provided on the screen that can do basic math functions (addition, subtraction, multiplication, division, and square roots). See page 169 – "Navigating the Electronic GRE" – for more information about what the calculator will look like on the screen.

The sections below will describe the types of math skills you will need to solve the Quantitative problems on the GRE. Sample questions will be given of different question types so that you get comfortable seeing multiple choice, quantitative comparison, and numeric entry questions. The practice questions within this chapter and in the "Test Your Knowledge: Quantitative Reasoning" section in Chapter 4 will include all of the question structure types.

We'll go through the math types one at a time, but you'll see that questions on the GRE often make use of multiple different math skills at once: to solve a problem, you may need to read a geometric figure, use algebra to set up an equation, and solve using arithmetic techniques.

General Strategy
The best things you can do to avoid making mistakes on the Quantitative Reasoning problems are to **read carefully** and **write things down**. You're allowed plenty of scratch paper, and you should use it. You may not need it for every problem, and you shouldn't waste time by copying whole questions directly from the screen, but for most problems it will be helpful to write things out and stay organized. In the explanations for the example problems given, I'll give the suggested scratch notes you should make. Adapt this to your own style, but organization and clarity are important to swiftly and correctly answer these problems.

The math in these problems isn't necessarily difficult, but questions are often structured to be maximally confusing. The wrong answer choices presented to you are given for a reason: they represent traps that many people fall into by not staying organized.
Remember, there is no penalty for answering a question wrong, so you should attempt every question on a GRE Quantitative Reasoning section. If you find yourself running out of time, guess on any remaining questions that you don't have time to answer.

ARITHMETIC

This includes the basic math functions (addition, subtraction, multiplication, and division) as well as understanding properties of numbers: how number lines work, what integers are, inequalities, and prime, even, and odd numbers. Let's look at examples of problems that use these skills, and how to solve them:

1. At an elementary school, the ratio of students to teachers is 24:1. If the school employs 17 teachers, how many students are enrolled at the school?

    Grid in your answer:

    17×24 = 408

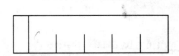

2. The value of a car has depreciated at a rate of 17.0% of the original value every year. A person who bought the car in January 2001 for $12,000 sold it in January of 2003 for $8,500.

    2003 −2400
    −2001 9,600 worth-yr 1
    2 yrs.

Quantity A	Quantity B
The value of the car in January 2003.	The price paid for the car in January 2003.

    9,000 (7,200 roughly) < *8,500*

    Which of the following is true, given the above information?

    don't do it for 2 yrs! You did it for 1 yr

    Right answer

    a) Quantity A is greater than Quantity B.
    b) Quantity B is greater than Quantity A.
    c) The two quantities are equal.
    d) There is not enough information provided to determine the relationship.

    6 15 17 23 24 24

3. For the following set of numbers {15, 23, 6, 24, 17, 24} the mode is equal to x, the median is equal to w, the mean is equal to y, and the range is equal to z. The relationships between these can be accurately written as which of the following? Select all that apply.

    a) $y < z < w < x$
    b) $y = z$
    c) $x > w > y$
    d) $w = 20$
    e) $z < y$
    f) $w = z$

    mode = most
    median = middle

    mode = 24 = X
    median = 17+23 = 20 = W / 2

    mean = average add #s together & ÷ by total amount

    mean = 18.167 = y
    Range = 24-6 = 18 = Z

    Range find the highest & lowest # in the set & find the difference by subtracting

4. $k < 0 < m < n < 8$

Quantity A	Quantity B
$|k|$	n

a) Quantity A is greater than Quantity B.
b) Quantity B is greater than Quantity A.
c) The two quantities are equal.
d) There is not enough information provided to determine the relationship.

[handwritten: ☆ |k| = absolute value]

ARITHMETIC – ANSWERS

Question 1: Ratios

In case you've forgotten, a **ratio** refers to things that occur in fixed quantities in relation to each other. For example, a recipe might call for a ratio of one tablespoon of baking soda to every two cups of flour. For this problem, there are 24 students for every 1 teacher. So, for every 2 teachers, there are 48 students. The two numbers, students and teachers, have to be multiplied by the same **factor** to keep them in the ratio. We know that there are 17 teachers employed by the school. 17 is 1 * 17, so 17 is our factor. To keep the numbers in the right ratio, we need to multiply the number of students by 17 as well. That gives us 408 students, which is the correct answer.

Because this problem is fairly simple, you may not need to write anything down to solve it. Let's make the problem more complicated, and see how our approach might change: Say that for every 24 students, there are 3 teachers. Now, how many students are enrolled if the school employs 17 teachers? There are several ways to do this problem:

Strategy 1: You can always set up a ratio as a fraction when you are solving these types of problems. To do this, you make the original ratio one fraction, and then set it equal to the second ratio, substituting in a variable for the missing quantity. Observe:

$$\frac{\text{number of students}}{\text{number of teachers}} : \quad \frac{24}{3} = \frac{x}{17}$$

[handwritten: 3×8=24 ; 17×8=136]

Now, you can just solve the equation for *x*.

Strategy 2: You can divide the first ratio by the lowest number in it to get a ratio of *x*:1, and then multiply to get your answer. We know that there are 24 students for every 3 teachers, a ratio of 24:3. To get a ratio of *x*:1, we can divide both numbers by three to get 8:1. Now, to find the number of students when we have 17 teachers, we multiply 8 by 17 as we did in the solution to the original problem.

The math in both of these strategies is ultimately the same, and they both work out to 136, which is the right number of students for this permutation of the problem.

Question 2: Rates of Change

A **rate of change** is commonly seen in problems dealing with interest, loans, sales, appreciation and depreciation, and investments. The important thing to notice is whether the value of something is increasing or decreasing. In this problem, the value of the car is depreciating, or decreasing in value, at a rate of 17% per year.

Unless otherwise stated, a rate like this is a **simple rate**: meaning that it increases or decreases by the same amount every year (or other specified period of time). That amount is the given percentage of the original balance, value, or principal. Let's solve this problem and then we'll look at how it would change if it used a compound rate.

The problem tells us the original value of the car, the rate of depreciation, and the number of years the first owner had the car. Then we are asked to compare the later value of the car with the amount paid for it by the second owner. Did they overpay for the car?

There are several ways to solve this problem, so if you approached it in a different way algebraically but still got the same answer, that's fine. We're going to go through the most basic method to answer it: bootstrapping the problem. "Bootstrapping" is when you work through lots of calculations step by step to arrive at the answer. It's not the fastest way to do a problem, but if you don't know a question's trick or formula, this will find the answer. There are occasions when bootstrapping is impossible due to the time it would take, and we'll address how to spot those later. Here, it's pretty simple, because there are only two years of depreciation to calculate.

Step 1: How much does the car depreciate each year?

We know from the problem that it depreciates by 17% of the original value each year. That means it's going down by the same dollar amount each year. To find that dollar amount, we just multiply 12,000 by 17%, or .17:

$$(12,000) * (.17) = 2,040$$

Step 2: What was the value of the car after two years?

So we know that the value of the car decreases by $2,040 annually. There are two years in question, so we just multiply this amount by two and subtract that from the original value of the car:

$$12,000 - (2,040 * 2) = 7,920$$

The car was worth $7,920, but it was sold for $8,500. The sell price, Quantity B, is greater, which is Choice B.

Compounded rate

What if the depreciation of the car was annually compounded? The question would then read: *The value of a car has depreciated at a rate of 17.0% each year. A person who bought the*

48

car in January 2001 for $12,000 sold it in January of 2003 for $8,500. Do you notice what changed? It no longer says "depreciated at a rate of 17.0% *of its original value* each year. Now we're dealing with a rate that compounds annually. All that means is that instead of changing by 17% of 12,000 each year, the value now changes by that much on the first year. On the second year, it will go down by 17% of the new value. On the third year, it will go down by 17% of what it was worth after two years.

Bootstrapping a compound interest problem is only worth your time if it only covers one or two periods, or timeframes (the period can be a year, like in this problem, or a month, a quarter, any unit of time). It would look like this:

Step 1: What is the car worth at the end of the first year?

$$(12,000) * (1 - .17) = 9,960$$

We set the problem up to give the value of the car, rather than finding 17% of 12,000 and then subtracting that from 12,000. The above equation just gives us 83% of 12,000, or the remaining value. You can do it either way.

Step 2: What is the car worth at the end of the second year?

$$(9,960) * (1 - .17) = 8266.8$$

If the car is depreciating with a compounded rate, it actually has *more* value at the end of the second year than it would if it were depreciating at a simple rate! That's because 17% of 9,960 is less than 17% of 12,000, which is what we subtracted from the value during year two in the original problem.

There is a formula for compound interest problems that you'll use if more than two periods are covered. What if this problem was written as: *The value of a car has depreciated at a rate of 17.0% each year. A person who bought the car in January 2001 for $12,000 sold it in January of 2010 for $2,500.* Now we're looking at the value of the car over nine years, and we simply don't have time to multiply it out each year.

Compound interest formula: $Value = Principal * (1 + r)^t$

Here, *r* is the rate and *t* is the number of time periods.

What would this look like for the value of the car?

$$(12,000) * (1 + -.17)^9 = 2,243.28$$

Our rate is negative, since it's depreciating.

The calculator you're given on the GRE does not have an exponent function, so this problem would likely end at the set-up stage. For example, you might have to compare the above expression with one similar, such as $(12,000) * (.74)^9$.

Question 3: Mean, Median, and Mode

Here's a refresher:

- The *mean* of a set of numbers is the same as the average. You find the mean by adding all of the numbers together, and then dividing by how many numbers there were. For example, we are told that the *mean* of the set of numbers given in this question is y. To find that mean, here's what we do:

$$\frac{15 + 23 + 6 + 24 + 17 + 24}{6} = y$$

We're adding all the numbers up in the set, and then dividing it by 6 because that's how many numbers we added. So we know that y must be equal to 18.167, approximately.

Sometimes a problem will give you the mean, or average, and then leave out one of the numbers in the set and you'll have to solve for that instead. You still set the problem up in the same way:

$$\frac{\textit{all the numbers in the set added together}}{\textit{amount of numbers in the set}} = \text{average}$$

If we use the same numbers from our last example, but we want to find the number 23 from the list of 6 numbers, the problem would look like this:

$$\frac{15 + b + 6 + 24 + 17 + 24}{6} = 18.167$$

We'll see some examples of problems like this in the Quantitative Reasoning Practice chapter.

- The *mode* of a set is the number which occurs the most often. In the given set, {15, 23, 6, 24, 17, 24}, 24 is the mode because it's the only number that occurs more than once. If there are two numbers that occur twice in a set, and no number that occurs more often than that, you'd have a set with two modes.

- The *median* is the number that comes in the middle of a set when you put all the numbers in ascending numerical order. If you have an odd amount of numbers, the median will be the middle number. If there is an even amount of numbers in your set, then the median will be the average of the two numbers in the middle. For example, in our set, when we reorder the numbers sequentially it looks like this:

6, 15, 17, 23, 24, 24

50

When you're finding the mode, you should always physically rewrite the set in order. If it's a big set, you should copy it directly from the screen, and then rewrite it in order, scratching off each number in the original set as you write it in the new ordered set. That way, you won't leave anything out. To find the median of this set, we'll average the two middle numbers since there is an even amount of numbers:

$$\frac{17 + 23}{2}$$

This gives us our median, which is 20.

- The *range* of a set is the distance between the lowest number and the highest number in the set. To find the range, you subtract the lowest number from the highest number. So, in our given set, the range would be 24 – 6, which equals 18. If the set had negative numbers, it would be even higher; for example, the difference between 24 and -6 would be 30.

Okay, so we've solved for the mode *(x)*, the median *(w)*, the mean *(y)*, and the range *(z)*. Our values are:

$x = 24$
$w = 20$
$y = 18.167$
$z = 18$

So which of the following statements are true? Remember, the instructions say to select all that apply.

a) $y < z < w < x$ Not true because y is greater than z.
b) $y = z$ Not true; y is slightly larger even though they are close.
c) $x > w > y$ True.
d) $w = 20$ True.
e) $z < y$ True.
f) $w = z$ Not true; w is greater.

So you would select answers **c), d), and e).** It's easy once you write it all out!

Question 4: Absolute Value
This is a concept that comes up in various types of problems. We are told the relationships between a set of variables, with some numbers thrown in for grounding purposes. We know that k is negative, because it is smaller than 0. The question asks us if the absolute value of k is bigger or smaller than the variable n.

$|k|$ means the distance of k from zero. If $k = -4$, then it is four units away from 0, so the absolute value would be positive 4. Therefore, we know that $|k|$ is some positive number.

However, is it bigger than *n*? We know that *n* is less than 8, greater than 0, and greater than *m*.

Let's test out a few values. Could *k* be -100? Yes; that is less than 0. If *k* were -100, then |k| would be 100. This is bigger than *n*, because we know *n* to be less than 8.

Could *k* be -2? Yes, because that is less than 0, which is all we know with certainty about *k*. If *k* = -2, then |k| would be 2. Is this bigger than *n*? We don't know. It's possible that *n* is less than 2. We only know that it's bigger than 0 and less than 8.

The answer is **d)**. We do not have sufficient information to determine the relationship.

ALGEBRA

According to the ETS, the algebra questions on the GRE include topics such as:

- Equations with exponents.

- Factoring algebraic expressions.

- Working with functions and equations.

- Inequalities.

- Setting up functions to solve word problems.

- Coordinate geometry: graphing functions and finding slopes and intercepts.

Again, these problems come in the form of Quantitative Comparison, multiple choice, and Numeric Entry questions. As long as you are comfortable working with equations that use variables, you'll be able to approach most of the algebra problems. In this section, we'll review general concepts that will come up on the GRE that employ these concepts. If you need a more in-depth refresher on how to approach algebra in general, you will find our recommendation on where to go for this in the "Free Additional Resources" chapter.

Let's look at examples of these types of problems, and how to solve them:

1. The value t is an integer for which $\frac{3}{2^{t+1}} = 12$. The value of t must be equal to:

$$t = -3$$

2. Given that $x^2 + 5x = 24$, and one of the roots of the equation is x = 3, then the other value of x must be:
   a) -8
   b) -5
   c) 3
   d) 5
   e) 8

Directions: Select All Answers That Apply:

3. The management of a hotel has decided to repaint all 52 of its rooms. Painting one room requires one and a half gallons of primer and two gallons of paint. The budget for buying both the paint and the primer necessary to cover all 52 rooms is $3,225. If a gallon of primer is one-third the cost of a gallon of paint and the project ran exactly to budget, what was the price paid per gallon of paint?
    a) $8.27
    b) $17.72
    c) $21.50
    d) $24.81
    e) $26.05

4. Along a coordinate plane, line q intersects point R (4, -9) and point S (-3, x). The slope of line q is 3. What the value of x?
    a) -30
    b) -34/3
    c) 1
    d) 11
    e) 12

ALGEBRA – ANSWERS

Question 1: Algebraic Equations and Exponents
To solve this problem, we must find the value of an exponent that will solve this equation.

$$\frac{3}{2^{t+1}} = 12$$

The trick when solving equations with exponents is to get the two sides of the equation to look more similar. Let's do this:

$$\frac{3}{2^{t+1}} = \frac{12}{1}$$

Now we can multiply each side by 1/3; we're trying to isolate the exponent expression on the left side.

$$\frac{1}{2^{t+1}} = \frac{12}{3}$$

Then reduce:

$$\frac{1}{2^{t+1}} = 4$$

Okay, now we understand a little better what we're dealing with. Here are a few basic properties of exponents that you need to remember:

Properties of exponents

- Numbers with the same base can be multiplied by adding the exponents.

  - $2^3 * 2^4 = 2^7$

- Also, numbers with the same base can be divided by *subtracting* the exponents.

  - $\frac{4^5}{4^3} = 4^2$

- When an exponential expression is raised to another power, you can multiply the exponents to solve.

  - $(8^4)^2 = 8^8$

- A number raised to a negative power is the same as the inverse of that number raised to the positive power.

  - (Just put it in a fraction and make the exponent positive.)

  - $3^{-1} = \frac{1}{3}$

  - $2^{-2} = \frac{1}{2^2}$

- A number raised to a fractional power is the same as a root, or radical.

  - If you see a fractional power, put the base under a radical sign. The denominator of the exponent fraction is the root.

  - $2^{\frac{1}{2}} = \sqrt{2}$

  - $8^{\frac{1}{3}} = \sqrt[3]{8}$

Let's go back to our example problem. Here's what we have:

$$\frac{1}{2^{t+1}} = 4$$

We are looking for the value of *t*.

One simple way to solve this is to substitute in the variable *x* for the expression 2^{t+1}. That gives us:

$$\frac{1}{x} = 4$$

$$1 = 4x$$

55

When we solve this for x, we see that x must equal $\frac{1}{4}$.

Okay, so now we know that $2^{t+1} = \frac{1}{4}$. Which rule of exponents does this resemble? A negative exponent results in the base inverting to a fraction. To what power must you raise 2 in order to get 4?

$$2^2 = 4, \text{ so } 2^{-2} = \frac{1}{4}$$

Almost there! We know that we need to raise 2 to the power of negative 2. How do we solve for t?

$$t + 1 = -2$$
$$t = -3$$

There's our answer. These problems can be confusing, and it's unlikely that you'll make use of the laws of exponents on more than one or two problems on your GRE. But there's no reason to be intimidated; once you understand the rules and have a little practice, algebraic problems with exponents become simple. Remember, they won't throw any math at you that you can't do with minimal input, if any, from your calculator. These just rely on a bit of numerical sense and reasoning.

Question 2: Roots of an Equation
In this problem, we are told that $x^2 + 5x = 24$ and that one of the roots of the equation is $x = 3$.

What is a root? When an equation, like a quadratic equation (one which describes a parabola), has more than one answer, each answer is a "root." For example, in the equation:

$$x^2 - 4 = 0$$

Both $x = 2$ and $x = -2$ are roots of the equation, because they both describe a solution.
In this problem, we know that $x^2 + 5x = 24$. We need to factor this equation to get to the roots. I'll demonstrate and explain the process, but if you need more help with factoring after you've read this review and tried your hand at the provided questions, you may want to check the additional resource recommended in the "Free Additional Resources" chapter.

$x^2 + 5x - 24 = 0$	First, let's move 24 over to the other side so that we're in proper quadratic form, with an expression equal to 0.
$(x + \underline{})(x - \underline{}) = 0$	Now, we factor: we're looking for the two integers that will multiply out to 24 and add up to be 5. This is the common setup for a quadratic factorization. If the original expression began with a $2x^2$, then we'd need something like $(2x + \underline{})$ multiplied by $(x + \underline{})$. Fortunately, the problems like this you'll see on the GRE tend to be simple.

$(x + 8)(x - 3) = 0$	We are told that one root is $x = 3$. That means we fill in $(x - 3)$ for one side of this factorization. Why negative three? Because to solve for the roots, you take each set of $(x + \#)$ and set it equal to zero. If $x = 3$, then $x - 3 = 0$, and the whole expression on the left side will equal 0. This leaves us with $x + 8$ on the other side, because we need another number that equals 24 when multiplied by 3.
$x^2 - 3x + 8x - 24 = 0$	If you have time, multiply out the expression and compare it to the original to make sure you found a good solution.

Since we got $(x + 8)$ for the other side of the quadratic, we set that equal to zero.

$$x + 8 = 0$$
$$x = -8$$

The other root of this equation is -8.

Question 3: Systems of Equations

There's so much going on in this question – gallons, fractions, dollars, rooms! The key is to convert all the information we are given into algebraic equations; it's the only way to work this particular problem. Let's parse this out:

The management of a hotel has decided to repaint all 52 of the hotel rooms. Painting one room requires one and a half gallons of primer and two gallons of paint.

This tells us how much paint and how much primer we need.

$$1.5 * 52 = 78$$

78 = Total gallons needed of primer

$$2 * 52 = 104$$

104 = Total gallons needed of paint

The budget for buying both the paint and the primer necessary to cover all 52 rooms is $3,225.

Now we need to define some variables. What are we missing in this scenario? We're missing the cost per gallon of primer and the cost per gallon of paint. So: *Pa* stands for the cost of paint per gallon, and *Pr* stands for the cost of primer per gallon. On these types of story problems, it's important to be clear and consistent with your variables. Write them down, and stick to them.

Now, this sentence tells us that the total cost of primer plus the total cost of paint for all rooms has to cost $3,225. How can we express that in math terms?

$$\text{Total cost of primer} + \text{total cost of paint} = 3225$$

$$(\text{Cost of primer per gallon}) * (\text{number of gallons of primer}) + (\text{Cost of paint per gallon}) * (\text{number of gallons of paint}) = 3225$$

$$(Pr) * 78 + (Pa) * 104 = 3225$$

If a gallon of primer is one-third the cost of a gallon of paint and the project runs exactly on budget, what was the price paid per gallon of paint?

What does this last sentence tell us? Now we have a way to relate the cost of primer, *Pr*, and the cost of paint, *Pa*, so we can write another expression:

$$Pr = \frac{1}{3} Pa$$

The cost of primer is one-third the cost of paint.

This is a *systems of equations* problem. That means you have more than one equation and more than one variable, but you can use all the information together to solve for each variable. Here are our equations:

$$78(Pr) + 104(Pa) = 3225$$

$$Pr = \frac{1}{3} Pa$$

Usually when you have a system of equations, the best thing to do is substitute in the value of one variable in terms of a second variable. In this system, we have a clear expression for *Pr* in terms of *Pa*, so we're going to substitute that into the first equation and solve:

$$78(\frac{1}{3} Pa) + 104(Pa) = 3225$$

$$26(Pa) + 104(Pa) = 3225$$

$$130(Pa) = 3225$$

$$Pa = \$24.81$$

Now we know the cost of paint per gallon! We can substitute this back into our second equation to find the cost of primer:

$$Pr = \frac{1}{3} Pa$$

$$Pr = \frac{1}{3} (24.81)$$

$$Pr = \$8.27$$

This last step is unnecessary, because the question asked us for the cost of paint. But if we'd needed it, that's how it is done! Note that the cost of primer is an answer choice: you have to pay attention, because wrong answer choices are designed to appeal to those who make specific mistakes.

Question 4: Slope of a Line

You might remember from math classes that slope equals "rise over run," or the change along the y-axis divided by the change along the x-axis between two points on the line. That is the relationship that we use to solve this problem: we know the slope, and we know two points but we are missing one of the coordinates. There is only one number that the missing coordinate could be, given the slope of the line. Let's find it:

Point R is at (4, -9)
Point S is at (-3, x)
They lie on line q, which has a slope of 3.

We need to set up the "rise over run" formula:

$$\frac{difference\ in\ y\ coordinates}{difference\ in\ x\ coordinates} = \text{slope}$$

You can subtract the coordinates of point R from those of point S **or the other way around**, it doesn't matter, **as long as you are consistent.**

Note that the missing coordinate is called "x" but it is in the y position of the coordinate pair.

$$\frac{x+9}{-3-4} = 3$$

Now we solve:

$$\frac{x+9}{-7} = 3$$

$$x + 9 = -21$$

$$x = -30$$

GEOMETRY

According to the ETS, the geometry topics that may be included in the test include:

- Properties of parallel and perpendicular lines.

- Properties of circles, triangles, special triangles, and other polygons.

- Congruent and similar figures.

- Dimensions of three-dimensional figures.

You will not be provided with a "cheat sheet" that gives you any kind of formula on the GRE, so you'll need to memorize just a few basic formulas.

In this section, we'll give you those properties and formulas, and then run through examples of the types of problems you're likely to see employing those concepts. This format is different than the sections covering arithmetic, algebra, and data analysis questions, because there's a little more to memorize in the geometry topics and it's better for you to have all that information in one place.

Intersecting Lines

These are important. Know well these two things about intersecting lines: they form angles which add up to 180° along each line, and they create two pairs of congruent (equal) angles.

For example:

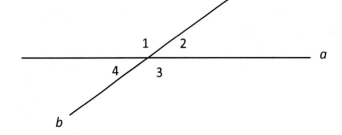

Line *a* intersects line *b*, forming angles 1, 2, 3, and 4. Any two angles along one line will add up to 180°. We know that 1 and 2 add up to 180°, because they are along line *a*. We know that 2 and 3 add up to 180°, because they are along line *b*.

3 and 4 also add up to 180°, as do 1 and 4.

We also know that angles 1 and 3 are equal to each other. They are "vertical angles." Angles 2 and 4 are also equal to each other for the same reason. If we are given the measurement of any one of these angles, we know the other three.

These properties can sneak up in all kinds of problems, so always look out for angles along a straight line.

Parallel and Perpendicular Lines

Parallel lines are lines that lie on the same 2D plane and never intersect each other. The main interesting thing about them is that if a line intersects two parallel lines, it will form a bunch of corresponding angles. Also, never assume that two lines are parallel just from a diagram; you need to be told or given enough information that you can deduce it. Parallel lines will have the same slope.

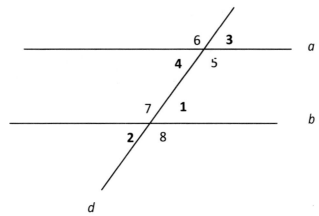

Lines *a* and *b* are parallel and are intersected by line *d*.

In this diagram, all four of the acute angles (the ones smaller than 90° - 1, 2, 3, and 4) are equal to each other. All four of the obtuse angles (the ones greater than 90° - 5, 6, 7, and 8) are equal to each other. Why? Because a line intersecting parallel lines forms similar angles. This is super useful: if you are given the degree value of one angle on the diagram above, you can fill in the rest of it. If one of the obtuse angles equals 120°, then you know all the obtuse angles equal that, which means all the acute angles equal 60°, since the angles along one line must add up to 180°.

Perpendicular lines are lines that intersect at a 90° angle. They are especially interesting in certain types of triangles, which we will cover.

Circles

The number of degrees in the central angle of circle is 180°.

The circumference of a circle, which is the measurement of the length of the outside line of it, can be found by this formula:

$$C = 2\pi r$$

Here, r is the radius, or the distance from the center of the circle to an outside point on the circle. If you have the diameter, which is the length of a line which runs through the middle of the circle and to two outside points, then you can find the circumference with this formula:

$$C = \pi d$$

The area of a circle can be found by this formula:

$$A = \pi r^2$$

Triangles

Properties of triangles include:

- The sum of the three interior angles of a triangle ALWAYS equals 180°.

- The length of any side of a any triangle cannot exceed the sum of the lengths of the other two sides.

- The area of a triangle will always equal one half of the product of its base and its height. It doesn't matter which side of the triangle is chose as the base; and the height of a triangle is the perpendicular line from the base to opposite angle.

For example:

In this triangle, the bottom leg is the base, and the dotted line is the height.

$$A = \frac{1}{2}\ (base * height)$$

There are some "special" triangles too, with additional properties:

- **Right triangles** are any triangle with one angle equaling 90°. The lengths of the sides of a right triangle can be found using the Pythagorean theorem:

$$a^2 + b^2 = c^2$$

a and b are the shorter sides and c is the longer side, or the hypotenuse. Also note than a and b are the base and the height if you are solving for the area of a right triangle.

- **Isosceles triangles** are triangles with two equal sides. They will also have two equal angles. If a triangle is both **right** and **isosceles**, then two short legs will both always have the same ratio to the hypotenuse, which is : $x\sqrt{2}$.

  For example, if an isosceles triangle has two legs with lengths of 4, the hypotenuse will be $4\sqrt{2}$ in length.

- **3-4-5 right triangles** are triangles with one 90° angle and sides in a ratio of 3:4:5. For example, a triangle might have a 90° angle, a base of 6, a height of 8, and a hypotenuse of length 10. These are common, so if you see a triangle that seems to fit the description, you can save yourself the moment of calculating the length of the missing side.

Polygons

Squares and rectangles are the most basic polygons. Here are their specific properties relevant to GRE questions:

- The area of a square is the length of one side squared. The area of a rectangle is the product of the base and the height.

- Each interior angle of a square or a rectangle is perpendicular, adding up to 360°.

- If you draw a line from one corner of a square or a rectangle to the opposite corner, you have two right triangles. If the figure is a square, then those two triangles are isosceles. This figure can come up in some problems.

Sum of the Interior Angles of a Polygon:
"Interior angles" are the angles that are inside a polygon. For example, the three angles inside a triangle all add up to have 180°. The interior angles of a square, parallelogram, or other 4-sided polygon all add up to be 360°. What is the sum of the interior angles of a hexagon (6 sides)? Or a nonagon (9 sides)? There's a formula for that!

$$(n - 2) * 180$$

N is the number of sides, or the number of angles (these are always equal). To find the sum, use this formula. So a hexagon has (6 – 2) * 180 = 720° degrees between its six angles. A nonagon has (9 – 2) * 180 = 840°.

If the sides of a polygon are equal in length, it is a **regular** polygon and the angle measurements will also be equal.

Area of a Polygon:
To find the area of a polygon that is not a square, rectangle, or triangle, you need to divide the figure up into squares, rectangles, and/or triangles and then add up the sums of those smaller areas. There's no way around this.

Congruent and Similar Figures
Be aware of this terminology:

Congruent figures are figures that have the same dimensions (the same side lengths and the same angles).

Similar figures are figures that have side lengths in the same proportion to each other. They will still have the same angle measurements, but the side lengths aren't equal, just proportional.

Three-Dimensional Figures
The 3D figures that you may encounter on the GRE include spheres, cylinders, boxes and cubes. There are usually only a few questions that touch on these, so brush up on the basic formulas but don't panic over them.

Cubes
The cube is the 3D figure where all the sides are perfect squares.

$$\text{Volume of a cube: (length of one side)}^3$$

This is why raising something to the third power is called "cubing" it!

$$\text{Surface area of a cube: (length of one side)}^2 * 6$$

The surface area of a 3D figure is the sum of the area of each of its sides. The sides of a cube are identical squares, so you find the area of one of those squares, and then multiply it by 6 since a cube has six sides.

Boxes
These are rectangular solids.

$$\text{Volume of a box: (length) * (width) * (height)}$$

Spheres

A sphere is basically a 3D circle. It has a radius, just like a circle: the distance from the center to any point on the surface of the sphere.

$$\text{Surface area of a sphere: } 4\pi r^2$$

$$\text{Volume of a sphere: } \frac{4}{3}\pi r^3$$

Cylinders

A cylinder is a figure with a base and a top formed by congruent circles, as well as a smooth tube connecting them. The GRE only asks cylinder questions that require you to calculate the volume.

$$\text{Volume of a cylinder: } \pi r^2 * \text{height}$$

Here, height is the length of the tube connecting the base and the top and r is the radius of the base and the top.

A Note About π

Sometimes answer choices are given with π as a part of the value; 2π, for example. When you see this, work out the problem by leaving the πs in rather than multiplying them out since you'll just have to factor them back in later. Otherwise, you can estimate that π is 3.14 or 22/7 in your calculations.

That's everything you need to know about geometry on the GRE. Here are a couple of sample problems, followed by their solutions. Note that there are more problems like these, along with detailed solution explanations, in the "Test Your Knowledge: Quantitative Reasoning" section of this guide (page 125).

PRACTICE DRILL: GEOMETRY

Question 1 Uses the Figure Below:

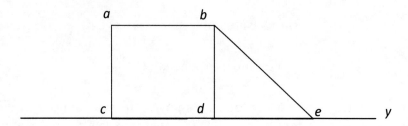

Square ABCD and triangle BDE both lay on line *y*. The length of AC is 8, and the length of CE is 14.

1.

Quantity A	Quantity B
Length of BE	12

    a) Quantity A is greater than quantity B.
    b) Quantity B is greater than quantity A.
    c) The two quantities are equal.
    d) There is not enough information provided to determine the relationship.

2. Circle A has a diameter of 26 inches. Circle B has a diameter that is 40% smaller than the diameter of Circle A. The area of Circle B is what percentage smaller than the area of Circle A?
    a) 22%
    b) 40%
    c) 52%
    d) 64%
    e) 84%

Question 3 Uses the Diagram and Information Below:

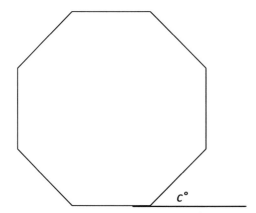

The figure at left is a regular octagon. One side of the octagon lies along line
l.

3. What is the value of c?
    a) 20
    b) 35
    c) 45
    d) 50
    e) 60

4. A decoration must be covered with foil. 8 square feet of foil is available. If the decoration is a cube, what is the maximum length possible of one side?
    a) .75 feet
    b) 1 foot
    c) 1.15 feet
    d) 2 feet
    e) 2.25 feet

PRACTICE DRILL: GEOMETRY – ANSWERS

Question 1: Lines, Squares, and Triangles

To solve this problem, we have to employ a few of our geometric identities. The first step is to quickly sketch the figure on your scratch paper in order to fill in what you know. ABCD is a square and the length of AC is 8 – that means that all the other sides of that square also have a length of 8. This also gives us one side of the triangle, since the two shapes share side BD.

The fact that the shapes lie together on the line tells us that the angles that meet at that point on the line will add up to 180°. Those are angles CDB and BDE. We know that CDB is 90°, because all angles in a square are 90°. That means that BDE is 90° as well, since 180 – 90 = 90, so we are dealing with a right triangle.

The last piece of information we are given is that line segment CE is 14 units long. We already know that CD is 8 units long, since it's one of the sides of that square, which means that DE must be the remaining 6 units long.

If you've labeled all of this on your graph, you'll see that the triangle is a special right triangle: its short sides are multiples of 3 and 4, so the long side, the hypotenuse, must be a multiple of 5. If you don't see that, you can quickly solve with the Pythagorean Theorem:

$$a^2 + b^2 = c^2$$
$$8^2 + 6^2 = BE^2$$
$$100 = BE^2$$
$$10 = BE$$

The length of BE is 10, so Quantity B, 12, is greater, which is answer choice **b)**.

Question 2: Circles

Circle A has a diameter of 26 inches. Circle B has a diameter that is 40% smaller than the diameter of Circle A. The area of Circle B is what percentage smaller than the area of Circle A?

The first thing you should notice about this problem is that we're dealing with circle area. What's the formula for the area of a circle?

$$A = \pi r^2$$

It's tempting to say that the area of Circle B must be 40% smaller than the area of Circle A, but look at that formula. The radius is squared, which means any change in the radius is going to affect the area by more than a 1:1 ratio. Let's work through the next step, solving for the area of Circle A:

$$Area\ of\ A = \pi r^2$$
$$Area\ of\ A = \pi (13)^2$$

Notice that we are given the diameter of Circle A, not the radius, so we have to divide it by 2 to use this formula.

$$Area\ of\ A = \pi(13)^2$$
$$Area\ of\ A = 169\pi$$

Always leave of the symbol for *pi* in your equations unless you get to the end and need a number.

Okay, now we solve first for the radius of Circle B, and then we can find its area:

Diameter of Circle B = 40% smaller than the diameter of Circle A

This is the same as saying that it is 60% of the diameter of A, so let's use that:

Diameter of B = .60 * (26)
Diameter of B = 15.6
Radius of B = 7.8

Now we can solve for the area:

$$Area\ of\ B = \pi r^2$$
$$Area\ of\ B = \pi 7.8^2$$
$$Area\ of\ B = 60.84\pi$$

For the final step of the problem, we want to know how much smaller the area of B is than the area of A, in terms of percentages:

Area of B = (1 − x)(Area of A)

We use "1 − x" to indicate percentage smaller; for example, if Bill's paycheck is 20% smaller than Tim's, then Bill's paycheck = (1 − .2)(Tom's paycheck). You can break this up into two steps if you're more comfortable with that.

60.84π = (1 − x)(169π)

First, we divide 60.84π by 169π. The π symbols cancel one another, so we never even have to calculate them out!

.36 = 1 − x
x = .64

The answer is 64%, which is choice **d)**.

Question 3: Sum of Interior Angles
We have a regular octagon, and then an angle across from one of its angles along a line. First, we need to solve for the size of each angle within the octagon. This means we need our sum of interior angles formula!

$$(n − 2) * 180$$

Since an octagon has 8 sides, the sum of its 8 angles adds up to:

$$(8 - 2) * 180$$
$$6 * 180 = 1080°$$

Since it's a regular octagon, we know that each angle is the same size. What is the degree measure of one of its angles? To find out, we divide the total sum by the number of angles:

$$\frac{1080}{8} = 135°$$

Now we need to know the size of the angle that's adjacent to one of the octagon's angles along a line. Remember that angles along a straight line will add up to 180°. We know that the octagon's angle is 135°, so to find the size of the other angle, $c°$, we simply subtract:

$$180° - 135° = c°$$

$$45° = c$$

Question 4: Surface Area
When a question is talking about covering something with something else, we know that this will be a surface area question. If a cube must be covered with foil, we're examining the surface area of a cube. Remember, the formula for this is $s^2 * 6$. That's the area of one side (s^2) multiplied by the number of sides. In this problem, the surface area cannot exceed 8 feet, because that's all the foil available. So how big are the sides? Let's set up the equation:

$$s^2 * 6 = 8$$
$$s^2 = 8/6$$
$$s^2 = 1.3$$
$$s = 1.154$$

We can round that to 1.15, which is answer choice **c)**.

DATA ANALYSIS

What the test-makers at ETS term "data analysis" really just means questions dealing with your ability to interpret given information. There's nothing in here that you'll have needed a statistics class to understand. Topics tested include:

- Data descriptors such as mean, median, and mode.

- Concepts of standard deviation, quartiles, and percentiles.

- Interpretation of graphs and tables.

- Frequency and basic probability.

- Probability of compound events.

- Combinations and permutations.

We've covered several of these topics in prior sections, but be aware that these topics can creep up in new ways in questions that deal with the analysis of information depicted through graphs and tables. In this section, we'll examine how the questions on the GRE present information graphically and how to address problems of probability and combinations.

Charts, Tables, and Graphs

Every GRE Quantitative Reasoning section will have a few problems that present you with data in a table or graph and then ask you questions about that information. When you see a graph or chart, you should always do the following:

- Look over the information presented, making note of the subject of the table or graph, any axis labels, and the general scale. You don't need to study the information too deeply, but you want to make sure that you have a handle on what's being presented before you move further.

- Note how many questions the information will pertain to – across the top of the screen, there should be a notification telling you "the information in this table is used on questions 3 and 4" or something similar. It's nice to know how long you're going to be dealing with this information before you get started.

That's all; once you've scanned the information being presented, you can get on with the questions. The questions will then ask you to find information from the graph and use it to calculate different things.

Let's look at an example.

The following Data is Used in Questions 1 and 2:

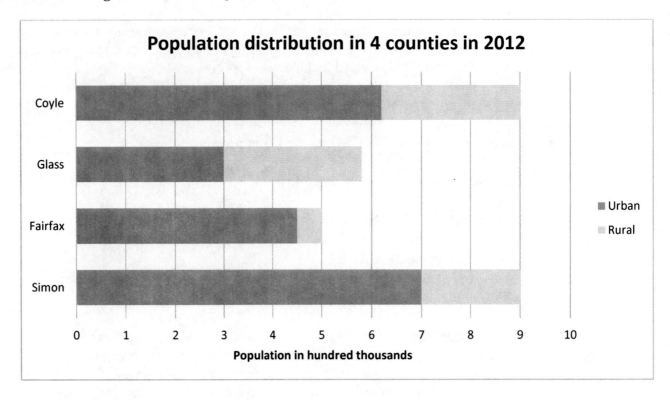

1. The population of Simon County has recently experienced a 20% shift to urban areas. What was the rural population of Simon County before this shift?
   a) 150,000
   b) 200,000
   c) 250,000
   d) 650,000
   e) 700,000

2. What is the total population of the two counties with the highest percentages of urban populations?
   a) 900,000
   b) 1,090,000
   c) 1,400,000
   d) 1,460,000
   e) 1,800,000

CHARTS, TABLES, AND GRAPHS – ANSWERS

Question 1
This question is telling us to look only at the Simon County line on the graph, so we don't need to worry about the other information being presented.

> *Simon County's population has recently experienced a 20% shift to urban areas; what was the rural population before this shift?*

You should always ask yourself what information you can pull from the graph to help you answer a question. What does the graph tell us about Simon County? Notice that the scale in this graph is a little odd: information is presented to us in hundreds of thousands, so a bar that extends to 9 really means 900,000. So we have a current urban population of 700,000 and a current rural population, 200,000.

How does this information help to solve the problem? We're looking for the old rural population. There was a 20% shift from rural to urban, resulting in the new populations of 200,000 rural and 700,000 urban. Let's use ORP to denote "old rural population."

Current rural population = 20% less than old rural population

$$200,000 = (1 - .2) * (ORP)$$

Remember, if something is "20% less than," then it is "80% of," since $100 - 20 = 80$.

$$200,000 = .8 * (ORP)$$

$$\frac{200,000}{.8} = ORP$$

$$250,000 = ORP$$

Question 2
What is the total population of the two counties with the highest percentages of urban populations?

We can use the graph to visually approximate which two counties have the highest level of urban populations as a percentage of the total populations: Fairfax and Simon Counties, the two for which the dark portion of the bar is much larger than the light portion.

Next, we add their total populations together:

$$900,000 + 500,000 = 1,400,000$$

Choice **c)** is our answer.

Probability

The probability questions on the GRE are straightforward. Let's look at an example of the kind of probability questions you can expect to encounter:

If a ticket is selected at random from a bowl with 100 tickets, then there is a .35 probability that the ticket number ends in the digit 5. A ticket selected at random has a .6 probability of being red. What is the probability that a selected ticket is both red and ends in the digit 5? Assume that the colors are evenly distributed among tickets of all numbers.

    a) .17
    b) .21
    c) .35
    d) .6
    e) .95

The probability covered on the GRE is very simplistic; a question like this is the most complicated that you'll find.

Remember that "a .35 probability" is the same thing as "a 35% chance." You can think in percentages if that's easier for you; just be prepared for the answer choices to be decimals, if that is how the problem is presented.

If there's a 35% chance that a ticket drawn from the bowl ends in the digit 5, we can assume that 35% of the tickets in the bowl end in the digit 5. Since there are 100 tickets in the bowl, that means that 35 of them end in the digit 5.

A ticket selected at random has a .6 probability of being red. Careful; that means there's a 60% chance that it's red, not a 6% chance! .06 would be 6%. So, following the logic above, we know that 60 of the tickets are red.

What is the probability that a ticket pulled from the bowl is red *and* ends in the digit 5? The problem adds that colors are randomly distributed; this just means that any ticket ending in 5 has the same chance of being red as any other ticket, because the problem says nothing to indicate that only blue tickets end in the digit 5.

What is the probability that a ticket ends in 5?

$$.35, \text{ or } 35\%, \text{ or } \frac{35}{100}.$$

What is the probability that a ticket is red?

$$.6, \text{ or } 60\%, \text{ or } \frac{60}{100}.$$

How do we find the *compound probability*, or the probability of both events happening in a single draw?

We multiply!

Anytime you want the probability of multiple events occurring, you multiply the probabilities of each individual event.

Therefore, the answer is .35 * .6, which equals .21, or 21%.

Combinations and Permutations
The best way to explain these problems is by doing them, so let's dive straight in!

1. A smoothie shop offers a "build your own smoothie" special:

> Choose any three ingredients!
> Banana
> Lemon
> Apple
> Strawberry
> Blueberry
> Mango
> Orange
> Coconut

How many different smoothies can be made using banana as an ingredient?

2. A casting director is considering a pool of twelve actors for three different possible roles. Each actor is being considered for every role, but an actor can only play one role in the production. How many different possible casting choices does she have?

The difference between a *combination* and a *permutation* is whether the order of the choices matters. For a smoothie, it doesn't matter whether we select banana as the first ingredient or the second ingredient; all that matters is which three ingredients will go into the blender. For a play, it matters who is playing each role; there's a big difference between casting Ryan Reynolds as Hamlet with Bruce Willis as his stepfather, King Claudius, and casting Bruce Willis as Hamlet with Ryan Reynolds as the evil, older king and this difference is important.

Question 1: Combinations – What To Do When Order Does Not Matter
The smoothie example above is a combination question. We can combine the ingredients in any order.

To figure out how many possible combinations there are, we multiply the number of choices for each slot by the number of choices in the other slots. Observe:

Three slots for a fruit in our smoothie.

_____, _____, _____

One slot has only one choice: it must be banana.

1, ____, _____

The next slot has 7 choices; the number of non-banana options left.

1, 7, ____

The last slot has six choices, since we already used banana and one other fruit.

1, 7, 6

Now we multiply:

1 * 7 * 6 = 42 possible smoothies!

However, this count includes such combinations as banana, mango, and orange; as well as banana, orange, and mango: that's really the same combination of fruit. We need to subtract out all the duplicate smoothies with this formula:

$$\text{Combination }(n,r) = \frac{n!}{r!(n-r)!}$$

Here, n is the number of objects and r is the number of slots or positions. An ! means a factorial. A factorial is a number multiplied by every number less than itself down to 1.

For example,
$$4! = 4 * 3 * 2 * 1 = 24$$

To do the smoothie problem we have 7 possible flavors (since we're excluding banana, which has already been chosen) and 2 open slots (since slot one is taken by banana):

$$\text{Combination }(7,2) = \frac{7!}{2!(7-2)!}$$

You may be thinking: "But I don't have a ! button on my calculator!" That's okay, because we can reduce:

$$\text{Combination } (7,2) = \frac{7*6*5*4*3*2*1}{(2*1)(5*4*3*2*1)}$$

Entire swaths of that expression cancel out, and we are left with:

$$\text{Combination } (7,2) = \frac{7*6}{2}$$

The number of possible smoothies, without the duplicate combinations, is 21.

When in doubt, think about whether the group of choices you've calculated has duplicates in it, and whether that is okay.

Question 2: Permutations – What To Do When Order DOES Matter
In the second problem above, the order in which each actor is assigned a role does matter. It is a permutation, whenever order matters.

For example, when inputting numbers into a lock, it matters whether you enter 52 – 16 – 64 or 64 – 16 – 52. One will open the lock and one won't. They should be called permutation locks!

To solve permutation problems, we take the approach outlined above, multiplying out the number of options available in each slot. We don't have to worry about factorials or formulas, because duplicate combinations are okay here: ABC is a different permutation than CBA, even though all the letters are the same.

If we have 12 actors vying for 3 roles, then:

Three slots for actors in the show.

_____, _____, _____

The first slot can be taken by any of the twelve actors.

12, _____, _____

The next slot can be taken by any of the 11 remaining actors.

12, 11, _____

The last slot has ten choices, since two actors are already cast.

12, 11, 10

Now we multiply:

12 * 11 * 10 = 1,320 different possible casting choices! This casting director has a big decision.

Now you've seen all of the Quantitative Reasoning question types for the GRE! Once you're comfortable with these topics, you should work through the practice problems presented in the "Test Your Knowledge: Quantitative Reasoning" chapter. This will help you determine which question types you may need additional practice with.

Just by reviewing what you can expect from the test, you've taken a huge load off of your shoulders for test day. **Congratulations!**

Chapter 3: Analytical Writing

When you take the GRE, your first task will be the Analytical Writing section. Before you attack any sentence completions or ratio problems, you will spend one hour writing two different analytical essays. Think of it think way: you'll get the hardest part out of the way first!

Regardless of how you feel about essays and writing, the Analytical Writing section can be cognitively exhausting because you have to dedicate your mind to the same task for a long period of time. After this section, you'll be able to take the GRE on a question-by-question basis, so, if you don't like a question, you can skip it and come back. The Analytical Writing section, though, is where you have to just grit your teeth and focus on each prompt in turn.

There are two Analytical Writing prompts in every GRE: one "analyze an issue" prompt, and one "analyze an argument" prompt. You are given thirty minutes to compose your response to each prompt. You have to submit your response to the first one before you will be given the second prompt, so: you have to write your "issue" essay first.

The two essays differ in content: your "analyze an issue" essay will build an argument in support of one side of a given issue, while your "analyze an argument" essay will critique someone else's position on a different issue. We'll look at examples of each, and how to construct a response to both kinds of prompts. Your execution of the two essays will be similar.

You will need to consider your approach to the prompt and carefully plan an outline. Your essays must be coherent; you can't write half of your essay supporting one position and then finish the essay with examples for a different position just because you think of them halfway through your allotted time. There are no right or wrong answers; you can answer in any way that you can support.

The process that you should use to approach each prompt is the same. We'll look at specific examples using this process in the sections for each essay type. The general Analytical Writing process has four steps:

Step 1: **Read** the prompt and make sure that you understand the question or issue at hand. Note any specific instructions in the prompt. Some might say "use well-chosen examples to illustrate your point" or "be sure to address any counterarguments against your position." These are tactics you should use in all of your essays, but if they are specifically requested in the prompt, you must address them. Take a couple of minutes to read the full prompt.

Step 2: **Brainstorm** points for your essay. You should do this before you know what your thesis will be, because your thesis is dependent on what great points and examples you can think of. Remember, you don't have to express your actual opinion in your essay. It's likely that you'll think of better points for a position you actually agree with, but this might not be the case. Give your brain a few minutes to dream up as many related points as before moving forward. The amount of time you spend doing this will vary from essay to essay, but in general you should spend about three or four minutes brainstorming.

Step 3: **Organize** your essay. Sketch an outline for your essay, since it is imperative that your essay has a structure before you begin writing it. **THEY WILL KNOW** if you are writing your essay on the fly, and the graders may deduct major points from your final score. We'll talk about top-score essay structures as we go through some examples. Again, the amount of time you take to organize your essay can vary, but the entire pre-writing process (including brainstorming) usually takes about ten minutes.

Step 4: **Write** your essay. Once you have your essay planned and your examples or points selected, you can concentrate on writing with good style and maybe even a little bit of pizazz. Depending on how quickly you can write comfortably, you want to make sure that you have about 20 minutes to do this.

Here's what you're aiming to achieve in every essay:

- A well-constructed argument.

- Convincing reasoning and examples.

- Tight organization.

- Good word usage and sentence structure variety.

- Appropriate length – Ideally five paragraphs.

Beware of Academic Dishonesty

The ETS will run your essay through software designed to detect similarities to published works and to other submitted GRE essays. Don't copy phrases from any published guides you read (including this one!) even if you happen to get the same or a similar prompt. Plagiarism will be immediately detected, and the ETS will cancel your entire score. It's okay to quote someone in your essay, but you must attribute the quote.

The Pool of Essay Topics

The entire pools of possible "analyze an issue" and "analyze an argument" essay prompts are published on the ETS website (see page 173). There are more than one hundred prompts of each type, so don't try to prepare an essay for all possible topics. However, browsing the list is a good way to assuage your fear of the unknown. If you read a sampling of each list, you'll see just how predictable these topics are. For our strategy discussion in this chapter, we'll use published GRE essay prompts from these lists as examples.

THE "ANALYZE AN ISSUE" ESSAY

If you took the SAT after 2004 or took the writing subject SAT test, this is likely the type of essay you wrote during that exam. These prompts will present an assertion about society, education, or value systems. They leave plenty of room for interpretation, and they will never reference a specific type of knowledge: bringing that expertise in is your job. Some of the topics are very broad, and others reference a specific societal question but leave the interpretation of the question up to you, so we will discuss both types of essay prompts.

Here is a smattering of "Analyze an Issue" essay prompts published by the ETS on their website. These prompts present an opinion, and then ask you to "Write a response in which you discuss the extent to which you agree or disagree with the statement and explain your reasoning for the position you take."[1]

- Scientists and other researchers should focus their research on areas that are likely to benefit the greatest number of people.

- Knowing about the past cannot help people to make important decisions today.

- We can usually learn much more from people whose views we share than from people whose views contradict our own.

- Nations should suspend government funding for the arts when significant numbers of their citizens are hungry or unemployed.

- Colleges and universities should require their students to spend at least one semester studying in a foreign country.

- The well-being of a society is enhanced when many of its people question authority.

Many prompts center on academia and the role of education in society, because it is presumed that GRE-takers have participated extensively in the education system. Others are generally about ethics and the structure of civil society.

Let's go through the process, step-by-step, of how to craft a top-score answer to these essay prompts.

---

[1] Source: ETS.org "Pool of Issue Topics."

Step 1: Read!

As explained above, these issue essays tend to focus on specific types of questions. However, there are a few different prompt spins that the ETS can give you, as well as some specific instructions that vary from essay to essay.

Broad, Vague Questions

These are the essay topics that make sweeping claims about some very abstract quality of society. What is truth? What is success? If a topic is so broad that you are having trouble answering the question, you can always narrow it into a specific context, or take a very specific mid-line response. For example, the prompt from the ETS pool listed above, "Knowing about the past cannot help people to make important decisions today," falls into this group. You might find it impossible to write clear-cut response, such as "knowing about the past *never* helps people to make important decisions" or "one must *always* examine the past to make an important decision."

You, as an essay writer, may need to sharpen the topic a little bit to come up with a defensible thesis. For example, you could write that "knowledge about the past creates a false confidence, leaving us unprepared for the challenges of the present." You aren't saying that knowledge of the past is always bad, but you're illustrating one particular way that making decisions based on past events can lead to downfall. Come up with a few great examples to illustrate this point, and you will have an awesome essay responding to a vague topic.

The greatest threat posed by the broad, vague question is that you may try to answer it comprehensively. **You cannot do this.** You do not have time. These topics have so many caveats and different applications. If you try to respond to the above prompt in a comprehensive, nuanced manner, you will end up with a very disjointed essay.

Can you write an essay in 30 minutes that supports this thesis: "knowing about the past is critical to making decisions today, but if we rely too much on the knowledge of the past we might fail to understand how our contemporary issues are different"? No, because it has at least two different components that need to be supported: knowing about the past is critical, *but* it can lead to a downfall *because* we might overlook how the present is different.

You want your thesis statement to be one strong, logical thought that you can then work to support through your essay. To make this possible, you'll have to narrow your scope a bit.

Agree or Disagree With a Specific Claim

These prompts do some of the work for you by outlining a viewpoint on a more concrete issue, such as a type of policy, and asking you to agree or disagree with that viewpoint. You do not have to narrow the scope yourself, because the question already does so. The prompt in the bulleted list given above, "Universities should require their students to spend at least one semester studying in a foreign country," is an example of this type.

With these questions, it's best to take a clear position either for or against the statement, without inserting too many caveats.

Which of the following is a better thesis for this foreign study prompt: "Universities should require students to study in a foreign country because it adds great depth to an education, with exceptions made for students in disciplines with strict timetables for graduation requirements and for students who have obligations outside of school." *Or* "Although the benefits of studying in a foreign country are many, universities should not require this of students because it does not fit in with every degree plan or life circumstance." The second thesis is clearer and easier to defend.

Read the Prompt Directions
Every prompt has a set of instructions following the claim. These instructions are some combination of the following:[2]

- "Write a response in which you discuss the extent to which you agree or disagree with the claim."

- "Be sure to address your most compelling examples and reasons."

- "And address those that can be used to challenge your position."

- "Consider the consequences of implementing the claim, and how this affects your position."

- "Discuss the reason (given in the prompt) on which the claim is based."

- "You should consider ways in which the statement might or might not hold true."

- "You should address both views presented."

Always make note of the instructions given with the prompt:

If you are told to address both claims, then you should have a paragraph refuting whichever claim you aren't taking or include references to how the opposite side of your argument would fail in each of your paragraphs, relating to each of your points and examples.

If you are told to address the consequences of a policy position, make sure that your essay does not only discuss the philosophical justifications for a policy but also how you feel it would affect circumstances in the real world.

Now that you have read the prompt, thought about whether it's a broad, open-ended question or a more concrete "take one of two sides" issue, and made note of any specific directions, you should move on to the next step.

---

[2] Source: ETS.org "Pool of Issue Topics."

Step 2: Brainstorm!

You should accept right now that it is unlikely that you will think of the *perfect* supporting evidence for your essay position during the few minutes you have to brainstorm. You might think of a better point when you have five minutes left to write. Accept this truth and prepare yourself to think of some pretty good, not necessarily perfect, essay points during your brainstorming session.

You have to be comfortable with moving on once you have thought of them, because you shouldn't waste time wracking your brain for the very best possible point to make. Don't hold your essay to impossible standards, especially since the ETS graders will not do that either.

You want to brainstorm before you've decided what your position will be. You may find yourself immediately gravitating to one side of a prompt, but unless you can come up with good examples and reasons to argue for that side, you may not end up writing the essay that way. Write down as many thoughts on your scratch paper as you can, and you can go from there.

You may also choose to brainstorm in the text editor provided for you to write your essay in, but you'll have to eventually delete your brainstorming before you submit your essay, which just gives you another step to worry about. If you hate writing your thoughts on paper, download the free PowerPrep GRE test simulator (explained further in the "Free Additional Resources" chapter) to see if you prefer brainstorming digitally.

Let's see what a brainstorm for a given essay prompt might look like. Here's one of the prompts from the ETS.org pool of "Analyze an Issue" essay topics:

> "Educational institutions have a responsibility to dissuade students from pursuing fields of study in which they are unlikely to succeed."

In a few minutes of thinking about this topic, here are some possible points and examples you may come up with:

- **Pro** – unemployment levels are high and need to prepare for the jobs that do exist.

- **Con** – structural discrimination – examples – women are thought to be worse at STEM fields, ex. Larry Summers Harvard quote.

- **Con** – too difficult to determine likely success, shouldn't base on high school class scores because some do better in a college environment.

- **Con** – already have grade policies in place which discourage students once they are failing in a field.

- **???** – does this prompt mean successful at studying the field, or successful in the 'real world' after graduation? how to determine success? gives too much power to the university.

- **Pro** – could save students money in not taking classes they will fail.

After a few minutes of listing out ideas like that, you should feel ready to try organizing an essay. Notice that this example does not use a "pro/con" T-chart to list ideas out for each side. You may feel that a T-chart is best for you, but the problem with it (the "con," if you will) is that T-charts tend to make people feel forced to think up an equal number of points for each side. They also discourage you from adding in other thoughts that are not immediately pro or con, like the example question above about what the prompt is referring to.

Organize your brainstorm however you like, but be aware of this pitfall and don't box yourself in. That will come in the next step. You want to use the brainstorming time to explore what the prompt means and how you can address it. Let's try brainstorming for one of the broad, vague prompts. Here is one from the ETS.org website Analyze an Issue prompt pool:

> "No field of study can advance significantly unless it incorporates knowledge and experience from outside that field."

That is a pretty broad, vague claim! Remember, on topics like this it is your task to bring in specificity and expertise. You can use whatever you studied and the fields of your interest to either support or deny this claim. Here is an example brainstorm for this topic:

- **Pro** – gains can be made much more quickly when people work together and share info.

- **Con** – some fields are very specific, example medical field.

- **Pro** – but advances in medicine are brought by physics, etc. – neuroimaging, radiation.

- **Pro** – all fields are trying to find universal truths and so work together.

- **Con** – specialization is required in this day and no one can be a generalist.

- **Pro** – breakthroughs tend to come from a shift in perspective. Disciplines offer different perspectives.

- **Example** – use of statistics to improve sanitation efforts.

- **Example** – economics/psychology/history.

86

Most of these example points support the claim, even though the claim itself is a little extreme. *No* field can advance without incorporating other fields? There are certainly many counter arguments to the absolute nature of that statement.

However, we can write a thesis that addresses this claim without spending valuable minutes and sentences agonizing over that problem, like this one: "Drawing connections between seemingly disparate fields of study is necessary to advance our understanding of the world because all fields seek to describe the truth." This thesis, drawing from the brainstorm above, supports the claim without needing to address the extreme aspect implicit in the prompt.

A Word about Examples
Coming up with examples can be hard. Fortunately, this is an aspect of essay-writing that you can brush up on before sitting the GRE. Spend an hour or two thinking about what you know well. Do you have an obsessive understanding of the history of a particular sport? Did you study literature, psychology, chemistry, or architecture? Have you recently visited an interesting museum, and do you remember a few details from the exhibits? *These can all be sources of great GRE essay examples.*

Think about books you've read, History Channel specials you've watched, sociological or scientific articles you've read, or interesting details from classes you've taken. Your examples do not have to be deeply researched or entirely accurate. If you can't quite remember a specific detail, just stay in the realm of plausibility to make your point. You aren't being graded on your facts; *you are being graded on your ability to employ facts to support an argument.*

A good essay will have two or three solid examples supporting your thesis. Your examples will pull from different areas of knowledge and human understanding, and each should serve to strengthen your case. We'll discuss how to do this in the next two steps of essay writing, but when you're brainstorming, you should remember to pull from all different areas of your expertise and understanding to find good, interesting examples.

The GRE topics are generally broad enough to allow all different types of expertise to shine through. You can use the same solid historical/literary/scientific examples that you can readily think of to support many different theses.

Step 3: Organize!
This is where you get to structure your essay. You may still be brainstorming a bit during this step, so don't be afraid to add new ideas and examples as you organize. However, once you stop organizing and start writing that essay, you'll want to stop thinking about ideas and start executing the ones you've already thought of.

Once you decide which position you're taking and you have an idea of why, it's time to start organizing. Or, if you have brainstormed for five minutes, you should start organizing, even if you aren't absolutely sure about everything yet.

This is the most important step, because the bulk of the essay scoring is based on whether your essay is logical and well-organized. What constitutes a well-organized essay?

- The thesis is easy to understand and takes a clear stance on the topic.

- The thesis does not just answer "yes" or "no", but gives a reason for the position.

- Each paragraph in the body of the essay has a topic sentence.

- Each paragraph serves to support the thesis in a new and clear way.

- The paragraphs transition nicely from one to the next.

- The essay anticipates and addresses counter-arguments.

You do not want your essay to have points that don't go anywhere or to bring up arguments that do not tie in well to your thesis. You want quality over quantity when it comes to your arguments; if something does not work for your piece, leave it out.

Let's use the prompt described in the brainstorming section, about whether colleges have a responsibility to discourage students from certain fields of study. Based on the brainstorm, we'll argue against the prompt.

First, you want to write a strong thesis. We have brainstormed a few ideas about why it's a bad idea to allow colleges to dissuade students: they may be biased in their thinking about the abilities of certain students, they should not use high school scores to dictate students' possibilities, and they can't determine what success means to each student or each field. What do these arguments have in common? What is the thesis? You want to find some core among your arguments to tie them together into a coherent statement.

In this example, the core argument seems to be: universities do not have the right kind of information to determine which students would be successful in which fields of study, and therefore cannot take on the responsibility of dissuading students. There is our thesis statement!

Once you have a thesis statement, write it down on your paper or type it into the text editor so you don't forget it. Remember, you are working under high pressure, so don't take any chances with your thesis.

Next, you need to organize your supporting paragraphs. Each paragraph should illustrate an idea that supports your thesis. Don't use each paragraph to elaborate on an example that supports the same point over and over – each one should support your thesis in a slightly different way. You want intellectual nuance, not fifth-grade-style structure. Let's see how this might look with our example:

- First supporting paragraph: Lead with the example you feel most prepared to write about, so that your subconscious can continue working out details for the next point. The topic sentence/sentences should be something like this: "Universities employ people who may have biases against certain types of students. If university officials are told to discourage students from fields based on their own assessments of whether students can be successful, these biases will systematically keep certain students out of certain fields."

You can write this down on your scratch paper, or type it into the text editor. Next, make use of your examples; you may cite research about bias, or quote Larry Summers, the former president of Harvard University, who stated that women have less natural aptitude for math and science than men.

- Second supporting paragraph: Here, the topic sentence needs to further support the thesis, but in a different way from that illustrated in the last paragraph. Let's go with this: "University officials may not only fail to judge whether students can be successful. They might also misjudge what success means." This further supports the claim that universities do not have enough information to accurately judge which students can succeed in which fields. If you can support your thesis from different angles, such as showing that universities cannot evaluate students *and* that they cannot evaluate success, this will demonstrate analytical sophistication.

You need a few examples for this paragraph; perhaps you can cite an anecdote of someone who did badly in a classroom setting but went on to change a field (the Einstein example is a bit overused, but there are others in science, technology and literature). You could write about how success in a field changes as a field changes, and universities may not recognize where a field is going or can potentially go.

- Third supporting paragraph: If you have a third strong point to support your thesis, this is where it goes. In our brainstorm for this topic, there are a few other ideas which could be used: the fact that there are already systems to discourage students who are failing, etc. However, if you don't feel that this point is as strong as the previous two, and you are running lower on time, this paragraph will serve to *refute the opposite side.* Including a paragraph to do this is almost always a good idea.

The topic sentences for this paragraph could read: "Some claim that universities have an obligation to steer students away from subjects where they may fail to prevent students from wasting money on classes and graduating without job preparation. Rather than preventing students from studying what they wish to study, universities should help mitigate these problems by offering quality academic and career advising services." Then you can go on to explain how the arguments given by the other side are not as strong as your reasoning. This is an excellent way to make use of the brainstorming you did before you decided what your thesis statement would be.

Take one or two of your opposite-side arguments, and then refute them. If you had an argument that you can't think of a way to refute, then just ignore it; don't bring up an alternate perspective if you cannot convincingly address it.

- <u>Concluding paragraph</u>: You do not need to really plan this out, unless you have a fantastic quote or sentence you know you want to end your essay with. Just tidily sum up everything you've said to argue your thesis.

Alternate organizational strategies:

- If you have three solid points for your argument, but you can't think of a good counter-argument, just use the solid points you have. Likewise, you can have four body paragraphs if you have three good points *and* some counterarguments. Just keep an eye on the clock and don't sacrifice a concluding paragraph, even if it is only two sentences long.

- If you are struck by a creative brainwave and want to approach the topic in a more narrative way, you can do that. You can use a personal anecdote, or open with something more narratively interesting. However, this does not excuse you from needing to demonstrate why your claim regarding the prompt is correct. Don't just tell a story and assume the reader will draw your conclusion from it. It's best to stay away from the narrative strategy unless you're very comfortable with writing and the prompt perfectly speaks to you.

Step 4: Write!
Once you're clear on what your argument is and how you are going to support it, you are ready to start writing. Honestly, you've already done the hard work by this point. All you have to do is flesh out your outline.

The majority of the points you'll get for your essay come from solid logic and good organization. You've already done this part. Now what you are going for are the points you can get for style and clear writing. While you are writing, remember the following:

- Only use words if you are sure of what they mean.

- Don't use extra phrases just to be wordy or fancy.

- Write in an engaging way, like you are speaking to the reader.

- But also write formally, like you are speaking to the reader in front of judges: no slang.

You won't lose points if you make a few spelling or grammatical mistakes. You only lose those points if your mistakes are so bad that they obscure your meaning. You are mainly being judged on your ability to construct a good argument, so the point of your writing is to let that argument clearly shine.

Below is an example essay for the topic we've been discussing. This essay would score a 5 or a 6 because it explores and analyzes complex ideas, it gives examples to support the reasoning, it is aware of counterarguments, it is clearly organized, and the sentences function well and contain some variety.

Analyze an Issue Sample Essay

The suggestion that universities have an obligation to dissuade students from fields in which they would not succeed rests on the assumption that universities would be able to accomplish this task. However, due to the skewing of information due to biases and differing definitions of success across fields and individuals, this is impossible. Universities are not obligated to take on this responsibility because they simply do not have enough information to do so, and never will.

Researchers have long examined structural biases held regarding different groups of people's ability to perform different tasks. Well-known biases include the belief that women are naturally less skilled in engineering, an appalling misconception that reaches the upper echelon. Larry Summers, the former president of Harvard University, received flack when he suggested this. The truth is that many of those well-established in academia hold similar views, and that this perspective has been proven by countless scientific studies to be wrong. If patently false misconceptions like this one still exist among those with power in the universities, how can we entrust university administrators to judge who is best suited for which field? Allowing this to happen would continue the ghastly tradition of systematically denying women, racial minorities, and those with learning disabilities from even attempting certain courses of study. There are myriad biases that might interfere with this process – the notion that men are not good with children and are not compassionate may keep them out of teaching and nursing, two fields which greatly need a wide pool of trained candidates. The ramifications of allowing bias to affect the future supplies of engineers, teachers, nurses, and many other skilled laborers could result in nationwide shortages.

In addition to incorrectly judging who is capable of succeeding in which field, people are also prone to misjudge what success means. For example, the typical definition of success for someone obtaining a Master's in Business Administration is that he or she will proceed to earn a lot of money. However, if more students who do not fit the traditional profile of an MBA student enter the program, they may go on to change the face of business administration and achieve things like creating companies with excellent human resource policies, building connections between businesses and communities, and expanding the definition of what success in business means. This is applicable to all fields – allowing students who seem like a natural fit for an arts program to instead enter chemistry might result in new perspectives emerging in the field of chemistry. Conversely, allowing a high school chemistry whiz to study art because he or she wants to do so could result in incredible new sculptural techniques. Sticking with the rigid definitions of what success currently means in each field to determine who should join that field will stunt us from developing across all pursuits. Advocates of a policy like this fear that students will waste time and money attempting a course of study which does not suit them. This is better addressed by ensuring that university students have access to great counseling and career planning services. We should be enabling students to determine their best course for success, not determining it for them with imperfect information.

THE "ANALYZE AN ARGUMENT" ESSAY

Remember the four-step process we used to write the "Analyze an Issue" essay? We use the same process to "Analyze an Argument." This part of the GRE is, like before, trying to test your ability to reason and understand the construction of an argument. However, this section is a little more satisfying, since we'll be tearing down *other people's* arguments!

All of the essay prompts we'll practice with in this section can be found on the ETS website, and they'll all give you brief vignettes of some policy or position taken by a given agent: a business, a school, a city government, etc. You will need to take this argument apart and evaluate it. Let's look at some examples from the ETS site:

1. The following was written as a part of an application for a small-business loan by a group of developers in the city of Monroe:

   "A jazz music club in Monroe would be a tremendously profitable enterprise. Currently, the nearest jazz club is 65 miles away; thus, the proposed new jazz club in Monroe, the C-Note, would have the local market all to itself. Plus, jazz is extremely popular in Monroe: over 100,000 people attended Monroe's annual jazz festival last summer; several well-known jazz musicians live in Monroe; and the highest-rated radio program in Monroe is 'Jazz Nightly,' which airs every weeknight at 7 P.M. Finally, a nationwide study indicates that the typical jazz fan spends close to $1,000 per year on jazz entertainment."

   - Write a response in which you discuss what specific evidence is needed to evaluate the argument and explain how the evidence would weaken or strengthen the argument.

2. The following appeared in a magazine article about planning for retirement:

   "Clearview should be a top choice for anyone seeking a place to retire, because it has spectacular natural beauty and a consistent climate. Another advantage is that housing costs in Clearview have fallen significantly during the past year, and taxes remain lower than those in neighboring towns. Moreover, Clearview's mayor promises many new programs to improve schools, streets, and public services. And best of all, retirees in Clearview can also expect excellent health care as they grow older, since the number of physicians in the area is far greater than the national average."

   - Write a response in which you discuss what specific evidence is needed to evaluate the argument and explain how the evidence would weaken or strengthen the argument.

3. The vice president for human resources at Climpson Industries sent the following recommendation to the company's president:

"In an effort to improve our employees' productivity, we should implement electronic monitoring of employees' Internet use from their workstations. Employees who use the Internet inappropriately from their workstations need to be identified and punished if we are to reduce the number of work hours spent on personal or recreational activities, such as shopping or playing games. Installing software on company computers to detect employees' Internet use is the best way to prevent employees from wasting time on the job. It will foster a better work ethic at Climpson and improve our overall profits."

- Write a response in which you discuss what specific evidence is needed to evaluate the argument and explain how the evidence would weaken or strengthen the argument.

The format in these examples matches that which you'll find in every "Analyze an Argument" prompt: you are given first the context, and then told to analyze the argument. Don't worry – the arguments are designed to have flaws, so you will never *not* have any points to make.

Remember: You are not being asked to answer the issue or question presented by the argument. Rather, you are being asked to evaluate whether or not the argument is strong.

Notice that the arguments do not touch upon traditionally divisive topics. This means that you will never have to analyze an argument which talks about an issue towards which you already have strong opinions. Instead, the arguments are constructed around banal topics like company or city policies. This has its drawbacks as well, as sometimes the issues are almost *too* banal – they can be so boring, you may have trouble concentrating on deconstructing the argument! But we'll help you through – keep these tips in mind:

Step 1: Read!
When you read your prompt (the argument), make sure that you understand the issue at stake as well as the argument's logic used. Before you analyze the argument, try to answer the following questions about the prompt:

- What is the issue?

- Who is making the argument?
- Which side does the argument take?

- What evidence is given?

- What specific instructions are you given in your task of analysis?

Let's look at the first example:

What is the issue?
Whether building a jazz club in the town of Monroe would be a profitable enterprise.

Who is making the argument?
The argument comes from a small business loan application. Or, in other words, the group of investors who would like to build this jazz club.

Which side does this argument take?
A jazz club would be profitable.

What evidence is given?
The nearest existing jazz club is far away. Also, the argument presents a few indicators that jazz is already popular in the town: a highly-attended jazz festival, the presence of local jazz musicians, and a popular radio jazz program. Also, the argument cites a statistic that jazz fans spend lots of money listening to jazz.

What specific instructions are you given?
You are told to write a response identifying what additional evidence is needed, and how that evidence would affect this argument.

And that's a basic summary of the prompt! We ask ourselves these questions as we're reading to make sure that we understand two things: what's going on, and what is the context for the given argument. If you overlook or misunderstand any of these elements, you won't be able to write a convincing response.

Step 2: Brainstorm!
The "Analyze an Argument" essay is less open-ended than the "Analyze an Issue" essay. Sure, you can get creative in your reasoning, but the task is relatively straightforward. However, you still need to develop a cogent argument which takes the logic of the prompt into account – no listing bullet points or presenting underdeveloped ideas!

You can analyze the logic behind an argument while brainstorming. Take each piece of evidence that is offered in the argument and ask yourself, "**How does this lead to the argument's conclusion? How might that logic be false?**" Ask, "**What assumptions are being made, and what pieces are missing?**"

Let's look at what the brainstorming process might mean for this prompt:

Evidence 1: The nearest jazz club is far away, so the new club would have the market to itself. How often do people go to the jazz club? If they only go once a month, they might not mind driving 65 miles. Or maybe that far-away club is located in a big urban center, and so it draws from a lot of business; Monroe's population wouldn't be big enough to create a similar market. More evidence may be needed regarding how often people visit this other jazz club, and from how far away.

Evidence 2: Jazz is popular in Monroe, proven by the festival, the radio station, and the musicians living here. Who is coming to this festival? Do those 100,000 people live in Monroe, or are they traveling from far away to come to an annual event? If they travel from far away, they won't be able to patronize a local club. The popularity of the jazz program on the radio seems like good evidence that there are jazz fans in town. We need more information though: what kind of jazz is played on the radio? Is it the same kind of jazz that would be played in a club? Who is listening? Maybe the radio jazz fans are introverts who don't like to go to clubs. Maybe a better indicator would be if there are other music clubs in town, and if they do well. In general, do people in Monroe like going out to hear live music? The fact that several jazz musicians live in town means only that there would be people to play shows, not necessarily that there would be an audience. Maybe we could ask those musicians where they've played in Monroe, and how well-attended those shows are.

Evidence 3: Jazz fans spend a lot of money on jazz entertainment. This statistic is too vague. Are they spending money on CDs instead of shows? Also, $1,000/year, if there are only ten fans in town, is not enough to sustain a club. We need more information about the total number of fans, not how much individual fans might spend.

What is the argument missing? There is no mention here of the cost of running a club. Has the loan applicant conducted a cost analysis? How much do jazz musicians charge to play a show?

Brainstorming for this is easier than brainstorming for the Analyze an Issue essay, because it's much more closed. You're simply looking for assumptions made and holes are left in the argument. If you can think of good counter examples, feel free to use them, but you do not have to construct your argument around them.

Step 3: Organize!
Which of the brainstormed arguments are you going to use? The important thing in this step is to ensure that you address each component of the argument, even if it is just to acknowledge and concede to it. It's better to say, "While the conclusion drawn in the argument is correct, it is resting on faulty facts," and then going on to explain why the facts are faulty, than it would be to simply address the facts and leave the reasoning alone.

Once you're sure that you have a plan to address each component of the argument, double-check the specific instructions. Are you being asked to provide a list of questions that must be answered before the argument can be evaluated? Do you need to consider the effects of implementing a specific policy? Keep those instructions in mind; you want to tie them in with each paragraph of your response. Be cognizant of what they are, and plan how you will address them.

That's pretty much it! The organization here does not need to be as tight as in the previous section, since you're attacking a given argument rather than constructing your own. Make sure you're ready to address everything, and organize response into the typical paragraph style rather than just listing all of the argument's problems. Pace yourself! Don't spend so long organizing that you run out of time to write a response to every aspect of the argument.

Step 4: Write!
You're ready to begin tearing that argument apart! Things to remember as you write:

- Only use words if you are sure what they mean.

- Write in an engaging, but academic, way.

- Address every aspect of the argument.

- Keep returning to the specific instructions you were given.

- Stick with an organized paragraph structure.

- Remember to have a little fun with these. You're tearing something down. Be vicious!

Here is an essay for the jazz club prompt. Because it is organized and well-written, while clearly deconstructing the logic given within the argument, it would score a fix or a six.

Analyze an Argument Sample Essay

It would be wonderful to have our very own jazz club in Monroe, especially one with a name as snazzy as "The C-Note." However, the only thing sadder than not having a jazz club at all is having a jazz club which only opens briefly before forlornly closing its doors. Before the business loan for this club is issued, two questions must be adequately answered: is there really a market in Monroe for this club? And, are jazz clubs profitable?

The hopeful proprietors of the C-Note have provided the bank with a list of facts intended to prove that there is indeed a market for a club of this kind. The first of these is that the only other jazz club in the area is 65 miles away, so jazz aficionados close by would prefer to have somewhere local to go. Before we can accept this logic, we need to know how well this distant jazz club is doing. Does this club have such a wide radius from which to draw patrons because the only way for a jazz club to exist in this area is to pull in customers from other towns? Are there towns to the east of Monroe with jazz fan residents which cannot travel to this existing club and who would be interested in attending one in our town? It is almost more distressing than it is optimistic that the nearest club is so far away; perhaps the area can only sustain one. We need to know whether that club is even doing well.

The loan applicants also mention our city's summer jazz festival, which draws 100,000 people annually. Surely they realize that not all of those 100,000 attendees live in Monroe; we need exact figures on how many jazz festival-goers are even from this state. I know Monroe denizens who prefer to *leave* town during the festival because of the crowds; this is not necessarily an indication that we have a year-round jazz market. The loan application also notes the listenership of the local jazz hour radio program. This is heartening evidence that we have jazz fans in town. However, are these fans the type of people who enjoy going to a club? Do they want to listen to more than one hour of jazz per week? Perhaps the radio station could announce the possibility to see if we get a public response. If these radio jazz fans are eager to also see jazz music live, then the prospects for the C-Note improve.

I'm not sure why the business loan applicants mentioned the fact that jazz musicians live in town, unless they are demonstrating that there will in fact be someone available to play the shows. A live music venue in a small town cannot be sustained only on the patronage of its musicians. However, these musicians might be a resource for further evidence of the demand for live jazz in Monroe: have they played shows in any venues around town before? Perhaps we could discuss with them what the turnout is like when they perform nearby. They are likely to have contact with many of Monroe's alleged jazz fans – this would give them a realistic view of the demand for live jazz music around town.

This business application is sorely missing a profit model. It is noted that jazz fans spend an average $1000 per year on their music, but there is no data regarding whether that money goes to shows, CDs, concerts, festivals, or their own shiny instruments. Also, most clubs profit more off of their food and drink offerings than they do on cover prices for the music. We'd be better served by an analysis of other clubs in Monroe which use music as a draw – do they tend to profit? What are the profit margins of those clubs? The likely market for this club may be those who currently patronize other music clubs in town, not those who sit at home listening to jazz on the radio. How much annually do Monroe citizens spend on going out? An analysis of this side of the business is necessary before we can consider funding the C-Note.

Chapter 4: Test Your Knowledge

You've come a long way, and refreshed a lot of knowledge. Now let's see how well you absorbed this information. This chapter will test you over the concepts which you'll need to know on the actual GRE. So get comfortable, and get ready! And above all, do your best!

TEST YOUR KNOWLEDGE: VERBAL REASONING

This chapter contains 40 questions (the equivalent of two full Verbal Reasoning sections). If you would like to time yourself, you should allot 30 minutes for each 20-question set. This mimics the form and pacing of an electronic GRE session. The question types are mixed as they would be on a GRE. The difficulty of these questions ranges from moderate to heavy. Detailed answers, along with strategy notes pertaining to the questions, are provided in the answer section on page 117.

For questions 1-6, select one choice for each blank from the corresponding box of choices. Answer each blank in a way so that all choices together best complete the sentence.

1. Her competitors accused the investor of ----- because her hunches were preternaturally accurate.
    a) Subterfuge
    b) Acumen
    c) Equivocation
    d) Proficiency
    e) Candor

2. Given the limited resources available, it would not be (i)---- to (ii)---- what we have.

Blank (i)	Blank (ii)
a) boorish	d) aggregate
b) expedient	e) relish
c) viable	f) squander

3. The short-lived poetry publication failed, not because the editors (i)----- to find an audience, but because they lacked the necessary (ii)----- of perspective to compete with the numerous other publications in the market.

Blank (i)	Blank (ii)
a) sought ways	d) ambiguity
b) were prepared	e) novelty
c) neglected	f) simplicity

4. The author was rarely intrigued by the ----- facets of detective work, preferring to linger over the moments of danger and suspense.
   a) Sensational
   b) Quotidian
   c) Effecting
   d) Copious
   e) Definitive

5. The Earth Day Network's ecological footprint calculator is a tool which estimates the volume of resources a person (i)---- in one year based on their living, travel, purchasing, and eating habits. The program then extrapolates this data to a global (ii)-----, informing the user when the earth's resources would (iii)----- the planet if everyone had the same habits.

Blank (i)	Blank (ii)	Blank (iii)
a) conserves	d) limit	g) recalibrate
b) sustains	e) meaning	h) stabilize
c) depletes	f) purview	i) exhaust

6. The reaction of the audience on the opening night was unexpectedly (i)------. After this (ii)------, the director of the show considered reworking the ending to give the characters more resolution.

Blank (i)	Blank (ii)
a) caustic	d) culmination
b) insolent	e) reception
c) indulgent	f) triumph

Question 7 is Based on the Following Passage:

Food waste is increasing in the United States to the point where last year, 40% of the food produced in the nation was not consumed. Consequences of this include wasted resources on food production, wasted energy on food transportation, lost nutrition in a nation with a high rate of food insecurity, and increased greenhouse gasses from the high levels of organic waste currently decomposing in our landfills. To address this issue, the State Counsel for Consumer Protection advocates a law requiring grocery stores and other food product retailers to take several steps to reduce food waste, such as: conducting waste audits on an annual basis, lowering prices on products which are nearing the end of shelf life to encourage consumers to purchase these products, and eliminating policies of overstocking product.

Directions: Select One Answer:

7. Which of the following facts, if true, would most undermine the intention of the proposal outlined in the passage?
    a) The bulk of food waste occurs after consumers have purchased food products.
    b) Stores which participate in waste audits are more likely to enact policies that reduce waste.
    c) Expiration dates posted on food products are largely not regulated.
    d) Agricultural practices result in a higher level of greenhouse gas production than food waste does.
    e) Food waste in the United States was already at 35% of all food produced only five years ago.

Questions 8-11 are Based on the Following Passage:

It is generally accepted among scientists who study the geology of the Moon, sometimes called selenologists, that the Moon was formed approximately 4.5 million years ago. Since the Apollo lunar missions of the late 1960s and 1970s, scientists have been gathering more data about the composition of the Moon, leading to several different theories about its formation. Two theories dominate conjecture on this topic, and selenologists await further evidence to develop our knowledge of the event.

One possible origin of the Moon is that it was elsewhere in the solar system and then captured by the gravitational pull of the Earth as it passed by. This makes sense given the composition of the Moon, which samples collected during the Apollo missions were shown to be 13% comprised of the iron oxide FeO. The Earth's mantle is 8% iron oxide, so it does not follow that the Moon is composed of the same material as the Earth. The gravitational conditions necessary to capture a body the size of the Moon are precise – it is much more likely that a body would collide with the Earth or pass by it, uncaptured. This is not evidence that it could not have happened; that is why there is only one Moon.

However, some do hold that the Moon was formed in proximity to the Earth, regardless of the difference in chemical composition between the two bodies. The giant impact theory posits that the Moon was formed when another planetary body, around the size of Mars, collided with the Earth 4.5 million years ago. The impact created a large amount of debris, which coalesced in orbit into the Moon. Estimates tested by computer simulations suggest that the debris could have formed the Moon within a month or within a century at the most – a trivial timeframe on an astronomic scale. Oxygen isotopes found in rocks on the Moon by the Apollo missions match those found in rocks on Earth, suggesting that part of Earth went into the composition of the Moon. Other compounds found on the Moon in greater quantities than on Earth can be explained by the other body, which would also have contributed debris to the formation of the Moon.

Directions: Select All Answers that Apply:

8. The chemical composition of the Moon is mentioned in this passage:
   a) To give support to the notion that the formation of the Moon occurred in a separate location in the solar system than the Earth was formed.
   b) To discredit the theory that the Moon was formed by a collision between Earth and another planetary body.
   c) To explain the process by which selenologists evaluate the merits of different theories regarding the origin of the Moon.
   d) As an example of data collected during the lunar Apollo missions.

Directions: Select One Answer:

9. Which of the following statements is most consistent with the lunar capture theory?
   a) The Moon has not been found to contain any material from the Earth in its composition.
   b) The Moon is partially composed of material from another planetary body in the solar system which collided with the Earth.
   c) The Earth and the Moon have nearly identical levels of oxygen isotopes.
   d) The Moon was probably formed around 4.5 million years ago.
   e) The gravitational conditions necessary to allow for a lunar capture are so specific as to be statistically incredible.

10. Which of the following discoveries would increase support for the giant impact theory?
   a) A planetary body, with the same mineral composition as the moon, in orbit around another planet in the solar system.
   b) Oxygen isotopes found on the Moon that are similar to those found on Earth.
   c) Material found on Earth, believed to be made from the other planetary body, which is similar to the material found on the Moon.
   d) The occurrence of Jupiter capturing a small, Moon-like body.
   e) Computer simulations which show that it would take at least a century for the debris from a similar impact to coalesce into a planetary body.

11. The highlighted sentence serves to:
   a) Explain why a fact used to detract from the theory discussed in the paragraph is actually a necessary condition for the theory to be plausible.
   b) Transition into the explanation of the second theory of the Moon's origin.
   c) Call into question the plausibility of the theory discussed earlier in the paragraph while still acknowledging that it may have value.
   d) Explain how a piece of evidence that undermines one theory can be used to support another theory.
   e) Summarize the theoretical perspectives that have been outlined so far in the passage.

Question 12 is Based on the Following Passage:

Blood types are used to describe agglutinogens, which are proteins attached to the surface of red blood cells. Those genes determining which agglutinogens a person's body will produce are inherited, and have three possible types: A, B, and O. An organism will produce antibodies, known as agglutinins, to guard against foreign agglutinogens. Depending on the types involved, this can result in adverse reactions when a person of one blood type receives the blood of a different type. This was not well understood until a process for typing the blood of individuals was developed in the 1930s.

12. Based on the passage, it can be assumed that:
   a) People with different blood types will produce different agglutinins.
   b) A person of blood type A receiving a transfusion of any other blood type will have an adverse reaction.
   c) Different types of proteins attach to the surface of white blood cells.
   d) Before the 1930s, blood transfusions carried a higher risk of an adverse reaction.
   e) The type of agglutinogens a body produces is based on several factors.

Directions: For questions 13 – 17, select the *two* answer choices that when substituted into the blank in the sentence fit the meaning of the sentence as a whole *and* create two sentences which are alike in meaning.

13. Although the experiment did address an issue raised by the previous study, it failed to substantially ------ the general line of inquiry.
   a) Resolve
   b) Further
   c) Investigate
   d) Develop
   e) Abase
   f) Revert

14. That French is only widely spoken in France is a -----; students of the language will find it useful in countries including Cameroon and Vietnam
   a) Bromide
   b) Misconception
   c) Truism
   d) Travesty
   e) Dissention
   f) Delusion

15. The automation of ---- tasks is much easier to achieve than that of ones which require particular finesse and judgment.
   a) Rote
   b) Convoluted
   c) Facile
   d) Inconsequential
   e) Minor
   f) Variegated

16. The tendency of travelers to seek small, unique accommodations, which has been facilitated by burgeoning global internet access, results in ----- market share for more traditional hotels but has heightened the profitability of the tourist industry overall.
   a) A thriving
   b) An opening
   c) A sinking
   d) A moderate
   e) A shifting
   f) A deteriorating

17. Around the time that female humpback whales are readying to give birth, their migratory patterns have led them to warmer, shallower waters: ideal conditions for the ----- needs of young calves.
   a) Premature
   b) Portending
   c) Myriad
   d) Imminent
   e) Explicit
   f) Upcoming

Question 18 is Based on the Following Passage:

Psychologists and those who study musical theory have long understood that successful popular songs share similar elements: verses, which have a similar melody structure but different lyrics each time they are repeated and which can serve to tell a story; choruses, which have a similar melody and similar lyrics each time they are repeated and serve to underscore themes in the song and to heighten the emotional intensity; and a collision, which can mix the two to create a narrative and musical climax. Listeners respond subconsciously to the repetition within the song, deriving pleasure from correctly anticipating the next beat. Surprisingly, the songs which become the most popular exploit this subconscious pattern-tracking by providing a narrative and musical twist that the listener does not expect. When this is done well, rather than aggravating the listener it provides a rush of excitement and surprise.

18. It can be inferred from the passage that a song would likely not be popular if it:
   a) Made use of verses, choruses, *and* collisions.
   b) Lacked a clearly defined narrative.
   c) Changed the melodic pattern in the final verse.
   d) Had a predictable structure.
   e) Included a twist in the first chorus.

Questions 19 and 20 are Based on the Following Passage:

Editorial letter:
The expectation in our society is that copyright laws should be preserved as-is, because to dismantle them would remove economic incentives to create and innovate and would encourage thievery. I feel that that it would, in fact, have the opposite effect. Community- and perspective-based creation, by which one takes the work done by another and filters it through a new lens or collaborates on a new iteration, is hampered by fear of reprisal under our current system. Thievery implies ownership – can one really steal an idea? Or should we move toward a new understanding of who owns knowledge, and how it can be fairly used?

19. The highlighted word "reprisal" could be replaced with which of the following words and still retain the meaning of the sentence?
   a) Theft.
   b) Retribution.
   c) Harm.
   d) Deviation.
   e) Progress.

Directions: Select All that Apply:

20. The author of this letter would likely agree with which of the following statements? Indicate all correct answers.
    a) The act of creation is largely motivated by the desire for profit.
    b) Collaborative works have more artistic value than individual works.
    c) A person's right to explore an idea is more important than a person's right to profit from his or her work.

If you are timing yourself, this is the end of one 30-minute section

Directions: For questions 21-27, select one choice for each blank from the corresponding box of choices. Answer each blank in a way so that all choices together best complete the sentence.

21. The joy of watching a dance performances is not derived from the technical proficiency of the dancers, the keen selection of the music, or the innovation of the choreography, but rather from how all of these elements --------- an exact temporal expression.
    a) Eradicate
    b) Are subsumed by
    c) Coalesce into
    d) Are served by
    e) Disperse into

22. The field of software design is characterized by a set of philosophical principles rather than rigid rules. Those who -------- the already established conventions fail to reach their inventive potential.
    a) Flout
    b) Disclose
    c) Shore up
    d) Dispute
    e) Adhere to

23. Erin (i)---- the volume of the music coming through her headphones in an effort to (ii)---- the conversation of the men sitting behind her on the bus.

Blank (i)	Blank (ii)
a) diminished	d) transcribe
b) mitigated	e) obscure
c) elevated	f) amplify

24. College students quickly learn that (i)----- can be much more valuable than (ii)------; all the intelligence in the world does not help if you are not able to manage your time.

Blank (i)	Blank (ii)
a) acumen	d) productivity
b) wiliness	e) ambition
c) efficiency	f) aptitude

25. Although the reasoning presented in the report was (i)------, it was based upon (ii)------ facts and thus was strongly criticized.

Blank (i)	Blank (ii)
a) faulty	d) misrepresented
b) undisciplined	e) verifiable
c) sound	f) irrelevant

26. The project team's habit of experiencing (i)----- stress in typical situations (ii)---- its response in times of emergency. These disproportionate reactions have resulted in the gross (iii)---- of time.

Blank (i)	Blank (ii)	Blank (iii)
a) thorough	d) primed	g) misallocation
b) undue	e) preempted	h) necessity
c) perilous	f) burdened	i) attribution

27. Biographer Anne Newell claimed that her insightful study of the notoriously opaque poet was simply the result of developing an ear for the way he talked. She recounted that after a long evening of discussion she would listen to the tapes of his (i)------ ramblings and (ii)------ the true meaning and emotion behind his performative words. The result is an account that differs very much from his poetic voice but provides (iii)------- clarity to his meaning.

Blank (i)	Blank (ii)	Blank (iii)
a) prolix	d) distill	g) irreverent
b) asinine	e) invent	h) fresh
c) laconic	f) cloud	i) reticent

Questions 28 – 31 are Based on the Following Passage:

Excerpted from Insects and Disease *by Rennie W. Doane, a popular science account published in 1910 (public domain).*

Yellow fever, while not so widespread as malaria, is more fatal and therefore more terrorizing. Its presence and spread are due entirely to a single species of mosquito, *Stegomyia calopus*. While this species is usually restricted to tropical or semi-tropical regions it sometimes makes its appearance in places farther north, especially in summer time, where it may thrive for a time. The adult mosquito is black, conspicuously marked with white. The legs and abdomen are banded with white and on the thorax is a series of white lines which in well-preserved specimens distinctly resembles a lyre. These mosquitoes are essentially domestic insects, for they are very rarely found except in houses or in their immediate vicinity. Once they enter a room they will scarcely leave it except to lay their eggs in a near-by cistern, water-pot, or some other convenient place.

Their habit of biting in the daytime has gained for them the name of "day mosquitoes" to distinguish them from the night feeders. But they will bite at night as well as by day and many other species are not at all adverse to a daylight meal, if the opportunity offers, so this habit is not distinctive. The recognition of these facts has a distinct bearing in the methods adopted to prevent the spread of yellow fever. There are no striking characters or habits in the larval or pupal stages that would enable us to distinguish without careful examination this species from other similar forms with which it might be associated.

For some time it was claimed that this species would breed only in clean water, but it has been found that it is not nearly so particular, some even claiming that it prefers foul water. I have seen them breeding in countless thousands in company with *Stegomyia scutellaris* and *Culex fatigans* in the sewer drains in Tahiti in the streets of Papeete. As the larva feed largely on bacteria one would expect to find them in exactly such places where the bacteria are of course abundant. The fact that they are able to live in any kind of water and in a very small amount of it well adapts them to their habits of living about dwellings.

28. Which of the following ideas would be a logical topic of a third paragraph in this passage?
    a) An historical example of the effect a yellow fever outbreak had on civilization.
    b) A biological explanation of how diseases are transmitted from insects to humans.
    c) A reference to the numbers of insects which live far away from human habitation.
    d) Strategies for the prevention of yellow fever and malaria.
    e) The differences between *Stegomyia calopus* and *Stegomyia scutellaris*.

29. The passage indicates that the species of mosquito discussed has all of the following patterns of behavior EXCEPT:
    a) Biting humans during both the night and the day.
    b) Traveling over moderate distances during the day to find sources of food.
    c) Laying eggs near sources of bacteria.
    d) Generally inhabiting tropical and semi-tropical regions.
    e) Preferring to inhabit areas with a source of still water.

Directions: Select All Answers that Apply:

30. Information in the final paragraph indicates that which of the following may be a method to reduce malaria deaths from mosquito bite transmission?
    a) Staying indoors during nighttime.
    b) Taking malarial preventative medications.
    c) Limiting occurrences of standing water with bacteria on the surface.
    d) Taking measures to eliminate the species *Stegomyia scutellaris* and *Culex fatigans* as well.
    e) Interrupting the breeding cycle of the species.

Directions: Select One Answer:

31. The author includes the highlighted sentence in order to:
    a) Mention that there are other species of insect which create the same problems as *Stegomyia calopus* does.
    b) List further characteristics of the life stages of the species which the author has been describing.
    c) Outline a necessary step in the prevention of mosquito-borne disease.
    d) Note a difficulty in the larger task of eliminating the spread of malaria and yellow fever.
    e) Call for the development of a protocol for the identification of disease-bearing insects.

Directions: For questions 32 – 36, select the *two* answer choices that when substituted into the blank in the sentence fit the meaning of the sentence as a whole *and* create two sentences which are alike in meaning.

32. According to his rhetoric leading up to the election, if elected, the candidate's supposed first priority would be to ---- the laws which were negatively affecting his constituency.
    a) Allay
    b) Sanction
    c) Abrogate
    d) Ratify
    e) Lampoon
    f) Rescind

33. In order to perpetuate the tradition, the family members made an effort to ---- the younger generation in the way that they had done it in the past.
   a) Assuage
   b) Coach
   c) Assimilate
   d) Reform
   e) Instruct
   f) Provoke

34. In weaving cloth with threads, one draws the weft, or horizontal yarns, through the warp yarns, or the vertical, in an even and ----- manner to create a tight cloth; deviations from this technique can result in imperfections in the final product.
   a) Consistent
   b) Oblique
   c) Erratic
   d) Uniform
   e) Substantial
   f) Tedious

35. ------ the law was to be expected, as the penalties for defying it were very harsh.
   a) Quibbling with
   b) Evading
   c) Compliance with
   d) Defiance of
   e) Compromising on
   f) Concession to

36. One of the characteristics ---- to my family is the ability to quickly adjust to any situation: my sisters, I, and my father are all this way.
   a) Diametric
   b) Alien
   c) Endemic
   d) Intrinsic
   e) Contrary
   f) Atypical

Questions 37 – 40 are Based on the Following Passage:

Adapted from A History of Art for Beginners and Students by Clara Erskine Clement, first published in 1887 (public domain).

Egyptian painting is principally found on the walls of temples and tombs, upon columns and cornices, and on small articles found in burial places. There is no doubt that it was used as a decoration; but it was also intended to be useful, and was so employed as to tell the history of the country;—its wars, with their conquests and triumphs, and the lives of the kings, and many other stories, are just as distinctly told by pictures as by the hieroglyphics or Egyptian writings. We can scarcely say that Egyptian painting is beautiful; but it certainly is very interesting.

The Egyptians had three kinds of painting: one on flat surfaces, a second on bas-reliefs, or designs a little raised and then colored, and a third on designs in intaglio, or hollowed out from the flat surface and the colors applied to the figures thus cut out. They had no knowledge of what we call perspective, that is, the art of representing a variety of objects on one flat surface, and making them appear to be at different distances from us—their drawing and their manner of expressing the meaning of what they painted were very crude. As far as the pictorial effect is concerned, there is very little difference between the three modes of Egyptian painting; their general appearance is very nearly the same.

The Egyptian artist sacrificed everything to the one consideration of telling his story clearly; the way in which he did this was sometimes very amusing, such as the making one man twice as tall as another in order to signify that he was of high position, such as a king or an officer of high rank. When figures are represented as following each other, those that are behind are frequently taller than those in front, and sometimes those that are farthest back are ranged in rows, with the feet of one row entirely above the heads of the others. An illustration of the storming of a fort by a king and his sons shows this. The sons are intended to be represented as following the father, and are in a row, one above the other.

One cannot study Egyptian painting without feeling sorry for the painters; for in all the enormous amount of work done by them no one man was recognized—no one is now remembered. We know some of the names of great Egyptian architects which are written in the historical rolls; but no painter's name has been thus preserved.

The fact that no greater progress was made is a proof of the discouraging influences that must have been around these artists, for it is not possible that none of them had imagination or originality: there must have been some whose souls were filled with poetic visions, for some of the Egyptian writings show that poetry existed in ancient Egypt. But of what use could imagination be to artists who were governed by the laws of a narrow priesthood, and hedged about by a superstitious religion which even laid down rules for art?

37. Which sentence provides evidence for the author's claim that Egyptian painters did not progress in line with their potential?

    a) The last sentence in paragraph 1 ("We can scarcely say…").

    b) The second sentence in paragraph 2 ("They had no knowledge…").

    c) The first sentence in paragraph 3 ("The Egyptian artist sacrificed…").

    d) The first sentence in paragraph 4 ("One cannot study…").

    e) The third sentence in paragraph 4 ("The fact that no greater…").

38. The word "consideration" in the first sentence of paragraph 3 in this context means:

    a) Estimation.

    b) solicitude

    c) concern

    d) contemplation

    e) reverence

Directions: Select All Answers that Apply:

39. The passage suggests that which of the following shaped the direction of ancient Egyptian art?

    a) Aesthetic concerns.

    b) Desire for realism.

    c) Historical record keeping.

    d) Availability of materials.

    e) Creative expression.

    f) Religious strictures.

Directions: Select One Answer:

40. Which of the following statements might challenge an assumption held by the author?

    a) There are several famous examples of poetry written in the ancient Egyptian culture.

    b) Ancient Egyptian art had to depict historical events because there was no other way to record them.

    c) Some Egyptian designs made use of both bas-relief and intaglio techniques.

    d) Ancient Egyptians found their style of painting more sophisticated than realistic art.

    e) The size of a figure depicted in a painting relative to the other figures was meant to indicate the importance of that person in civil life.

TEST YOUR KNOWLEDGE: VERBAL REASONING—ANSWERS

1. a).

After reading this sentence, we should understand that the word will be something negative – it's an accusation. The description "unrealistically accurate hunches in investing" implies that she's being accused of fraud, so we want a word that means something like that. *Acumen, proficiency,* and *candor* are all positive words; and *equivocation* means vagueness, which is bad but not fraudulent. *Subterfuge* is the best choice.

2. b) and f).

Read the full sentence first before looking at the blank. While we know that there are shortages of resources, we do have *some*. It's difficult to come up with words to fill in for this sentence off the top of your head, so don't waste time – go on to the answer choices. Since each word seems like a reasoning fit on its own, the trick is finding two words which work together in this context. If we select *boorish*, which means rude, for the first blank, which of the words for blank (ii) would work? *Relish* seems like it would work – but wait, it would NOT be boorish to relish what we have? When others are lacking? We must eliminate *boorish* because no word in column two works to complete the sentence adequately. *Viable* means possible, which might work if there were a word in column two which means "to increase" or something similar, but there is not. Therefore, we're stuck with *expedient*, which means practical. Given that, *squander* is the best complement.

3. c) and e).

First, we read the sentence. A magazine has failed, not for lack of an audience but because of something to do with its perspective. Okay, so we know that the word in the first blank must be something negative – it's a reason that a magazine might fail. "Failed to" find an audience would work. The second blank needs to describe the type of perspective that would be necessary to sustain a magazine in a crowded market, so it must be a positive word. Okay, let's look at the blanks. *Sought ways* and *were prepared* to find an audience are the opposite of what we want. *Neglected* is the correct answer in column (i). We can eliminate *ambiguity* in column (ii), because that's not necessarily a positive descriptor of a perspective. *Novelty* works better than *simplicity* when describing a way to stand out amid "numerous other publications."

4. b).

So the author prefers exciting, suspenseful moments over the -----. We are looking for a word that means the opposite of exciting: boring. That eliminates all answer choices except **b)**, *quotidian*, which means normal everyday facets.

5. c), f), and i).

A three-parter! You'll usually see a couple of these on each GRE Verbal Reasoning section. It's important to read the whole text before looking at the answers, because sometimes a sentence later in the text illuminates what we're looking for in the earlier blanks. This text is about a tool that allows people to estimate their resource footprint, and then gives them information about what would happen if everyone worldwide had

116

the same footprint. We can understand this from the text without filling in any blanks. Blank (i): it is initially unclear whether we are looking for a word that means "uses" or a word that means "saves." Once we've read the whole text, however, we can see that resources are running out. So we want a word that means "uses," which eliminates *conserves* and *sustains*. For Blank (ii), we want a word similar to "scale:" something that means we're now looking at resource consumption globally. *Limit* does not really fit this idea. *Meaning* is okay, but *purview* means scope or scale and is a much better fit. Finally, for Blank (iii), we're looking for something that means "run out." We can assume this because we're talking about resource use and a timeline. *Exhaust* fits best.

6. **a) and e).**
What kind of audience reaction would have a director consider rewriting a show? Probably a negative one. That eliminates *indulgent* from Column (i). *Caustic* and *insolent* are both negative words; which one better fits the context of an audience reaction to a show? *Insolent* means rude or ungrateful, while *caustic* means harsh or scathing. *Caustic* makes more sense, because *insolent* generally describes someone in a position with less power, like a child or a minion. Audience members have a lot of power over a show. For Blank (ii), we just want some word describing the event. *Culmination* means ending, and thus would not work for an opening night. *Triumph* certainly does not describe what has happened. *Reception* is a neutral word, but it works better than the rest.

7. **a).**
The intention of the proposal is to reduce food waste substantially by imposing regulation at the retailer level. If the worst waste occurs at the consumer level in the home, then this proposal will not address the problem outlined. Answer choice **b)** is further evidence in support of the proposal. Choice **c)** is sort of irrelevant. Choice **d)** indicates that other problems could be causing the effects that the proposal discusses, but increased greenhouse gas is only one ill effect of food waste mentioned in the passage. Choice **e)** is irrelevant to the logic of the passage.

8. **a) and d).**
We can eliminate answer choice B because there is never a presentation of evidence to discredit the impact theory. In the passage, the two theories are presented, but neither is discredited. We can eliminate choice **c)** because that process is not discussed in the passage. The passage gives evidence in support of different theories, but it does not discuss the dialogue among selenologists and the processes they use. Choice **a)** is true because the paragraph supporting the lunar capture theory presents the composition of the moon as possible supporting evidence, and **d)** is true because the passage mentions that the Apollo missions added to our knowledge of the Moon and later clarifies that this included the discovery of the composition of the Moon.

9. **a).**
We're looking for a statement that supports this theory: the Moon was formed elsewhere from the Earth and then captured by gravity into Earth's orbit. Choice **a)** supports the proposition that the Moon is not partially-formed from the same material as the Earth, which would be more consistent with the impact theory. In answering these questions,

you must be clear on the two separate theories. Try summarizing them each in one sentence before you answer a question like this one.

10. b).
Again, you need to be clear on the basis of the giant impact theory, which states that the Moon was formed when an unknown third body impacted the Earth and the resultant debris consolidated into the Moon. Evidence supporting that theory would show that the Moon was made from material from the Earth *and* from a third planetary body, which is why choice **c)** is not correct – it would undermine the role of the third body in the theory. **a)** and **d)** provide support for the lunar capture theory, and **e)** is irrelevant.

11. a).
It is important to understand the argument made at the end of the paragraph in question. The conditions needed to "capture" the Moon gravitationally are very, very particular. Detractors of the lunar capture theory use this to support their claim that this is an unlikely theory. However, proponents of the theory use this to their advantage, claiming the Earth does not have multiple Moons *because* the lunar capture theory is so unlikely. This is consistent with the description in answer choice **a)**.

12. d).
Here, we can eliminate the bad answers. Choice **a)** is tempting, but incorrect; the passage states that blood types describe the agglutinogens a body produces. It never states that the body produces different agglutinins. Those are different words. Choice **b)** is also tempting, but the passage states that adverse reactions are "dependent on the types involved." We don't have enough information to know that **b)** is true. Choice **c)** is too off-topic, as the passage never mentions white blood cells. Choice **d)** is good because we know that the blood typing test was developed in the '30s and that adverse reactions occur from mismatched blood types; it stands to reason that accurate typing would reduce the chance of adverse reactions. Choice **e)** can be eliminated because the passage only discusses one factor for the production of agglutinogens and does not tell us if there are additional factors.

13. b) and d).
Remember that the goal for these questions is to find two words which fit the sentence *and produce sentences alike in meaning. Resolve* and *investigate* sort of work, but they do not mean the same thing as any other answer choices and thus cannot be selected. *Abase* and *revert* are both negative words, and we know from the first sentence that we need a positive word. The sentence states that *although* the report achieved one positive thing, it failed to do something else. That word *although* signals that the sentence is reversing direction. We would not say that although it answered some questions, it failed to be a terrible report. *Although* is signaling that it failed in achieving the second good thing; in this case, furthering the general line of inquiry.

14. b) and d).

The sentence gives a statement about French, and then directly contradicts that statement. If the second statement is true, then the first must be a lie. Which words come closest to meaning a lie, or a false idea? *Misconception* and *delusion* both mean that something is a falsely believed idea, so those are our best answers.

15. a) and c).

This statement is telling us that it is much easier to automate one kind of task than the other kind, which is more complicated. What is the opposite of complicated? Simple. The two words which are closest to *simple* and are alike in meaning are *rote* and *facile*. *Convoluted* and *variegated* both imply complexity. *Inconsequential* does not mean that a task is simple, only unimportant. Something can be very difficult and still be inconsequential, *and the same goes for* m*inor*.

16. c) and f).

Choice **e)** could work, but as there is no other word on the list which would create a sentence alike in meaning, it cannot be a correct answer. The sentence is stating that small, unique accommodations are on the rise, so it would make sense for the market share of large and traditional hotels to be falling in response.

17. d) and f).

We are looking for a word that means "upcoming," because the whales are about to give birth. *Upcoming* is an answer choice, and *imminent* is the synonym on this list. Baby whales (calves) may have myriad needs, but there is no synonym to this word on the list.

18. e).

The passage states that musical and narrative twists are satisfying, if done well, at the *end* of a song, implying that a twist at the beginning of the song would aggravate a listener and fail to establish a pattern. Answer choices A, C, and D all describe elements of popular songs, and the passage never states that narration is necessary in popular music, eliminating choice B.

19. b).

Retribution means revenge or consequence for an action, as does *reprisal*.

20. b) and c).

The author is advocating the loosening of copyright laws in order to increase collaboration and creativity, on the philosophical grounds that knowledge cannot be owned. These ideas are explicitly stated in the text. Answer choice **a)**, on the other hand, is an argument for copyright laws, which the author rejects.

21. c).

First, we read the sentence. It describes many different elements of a performance and then states that they do something to create joy. What is an "exact temporal expression?" It seems to mean the artistic vision is created when all the different elements – music, dance, choreography – come together in a certain way. We should look for an answer choice that means this. Choice **c)** is the only one which does.

22. e).

The sentence tells us that software design has principles rather than rules. Because of this, we can assume that failure would come from sticking too closely to what has already been done. *Adhere to* means to stick rigidly to. *Flout* and *dispute* both mean that someone is challenging or ignoring the rules, which seems like a way to succeed in reaching creative potential. *Disclose* and *shore up* (which means to bolster) are not very relevant choices. Remember, we want the choices which are simple and direct.

23. c) and e).

It is unclear what's happening just from reading the sentence – either she wants to raise her volume to drown out the conversation, or she wants to lower her volume to overhear the conversation. Let's look at the answer choices to see which is possible. In column (i), both of those are options – we have *diminished* and *elevated* (we can eliminate *mitigated*). In column (ii), however, there is not a choice which clearly means *overhear*. *Amplify* means to make louder, but she's not making these men talk louder just by turning down her music. The best choice, then, is to go with **c)** and **e)**.

24. c) and f).

For the first blank, we need a word that means *organization*. Based on the clarifying statement after the semicolon, a word meaning *intelligence* ought to be placed in the second blank. These are straightforwardly options **c)** and **f)**. The biggest mistake to make on this question is to accidentally switch them around, and choose *acumen*, which means aptitude, for blank (i) and *productivity*, which is similar to *efficiency*, for blank (ii). However, by paying attention to the order of the original statement, that mistake can be avoided.

25. c) and d).

This sentence has two logical identifiers: *although* and *thus*. Remember, *although* means that the outcome you would expect did not happen. *Thus* means therefore. So we can see that since the outcome was criticism, the first part of the sentence should make it seem that this was an unexpected outcome. The description of the reasoning should be positive because of this structure. The reason the report was criticized is given with the second blank – something is wrong with the facts used to build the reasoning. *Misrepresented* is the best choice here. *Verifiable* is a *good* thing for facts to be. *Irrelevant* is negative but, since we know that the facts were used to build a reasonable case, does not make as much sense in the sentence.

26. b), e), and g).

The key word in this text is *disproportionate*. We know that the team is responding badly to both everyday situations and to emergencies. What is a bad response to a typical situation? Experiencing *undue*, or unnecessary, stress. What about a bad response to an actual emergency? A *preempted*, or obstructed, response. These two bad habits would lead to the wasting or misuse of time; *misallocation* works well here.

27. a), d), and h).

From reading the text, we get the impression that the poet is *opaque*, which means indirect, but the biographer has managed to get some direct meaning out of him for her biography. Blank (i) describes the way the poet speaks. *Laconic* means terse, which does not go with "ramblings" and can therefore be eliminated. *Asinine* means stupid; nothing in the text gives the impression that the poet is stupid. That leaves us with *prolix*, which is the correct answer. It means wordy or long-winded, but even if you didn't know that you may have gotten there by elimination. Blank (ii) describes how the biographer found the true meaning in his rambling words. *Distill* is exactly the right word here; it means to sift through a lot of something and extract the essence of it. What about the last sentence: the biography is different from the poet's work, but provides clarity to his meaning? What kind of clarity? *Fresh* works best, and is backed up by the *insightful* descriptor of the biography in the first sentence. Both indicate that she is providing new knowledge of this poet.

28. d).

The topics covered by the passage include: the link between disease and this species of mosquito; the habits and characteristics of the mosquito; and an emphasis on the proximity of the mosquito to humans. Choice **a)** is incorrect because the passage does not have any prior reference to human civilization on this scale nor mentions of epidemics. Choice **b)** is tempting, but not the best answer, because the biology of the passage is limited to organism larval stages; it does not get into the cellular level of disease transmission. Choices **c)** and **e)** are only tangentially relevant to the passage. Only Choice **d)** logically follows the discussion of the disease problem and mosquito habits.

29. b).

Every other choice is explicitly supported in the passage; however, **b)** is contradicted by the statement: "Once they enter a room they will scarcely leave it…"

30. c) and e).

The final paragraph discusses the breeding and feeding habits of mosquitos, noting that they lay their eggs in still, bacteria-laden water. Choice **c)** directly utilizes this information. Choice **e)** is the mechanism by which this would reduce malarial deaths: if standing water were removed, then mosquitos would not have a place near humans to lay their eggs. Choice **d)** is not a good answer choice. Choice **a)** is contradicted by the passage, which asserts that mosquitos bite during both day and night and can be found indoors. Choice **b)** might work, but it is never mentioned in the passage.

31. d).

The second paragraph notes the habits of mosquitos in order to halt the spread of malaria; and this sentence mentions that at several life stages, the species is indistinguishable from other species which do not cause malaria.

32. c) and f).

From reading the sentence, we can tell that the politician has been making campaign promises – it would make sense that he promises to get rid of laws that are harming his constituency. So we are looking for the two words that mean "get rid of." *Allay* means to alleviate or dispel – it's sort of on the right track, but doesn't necessarily fit with the idea of getting rid of a law. Rather, you would allay the bad effects of a law. *Sanction* and ratify mean to endorse or agree with, which is the opposite of what we want. *Lampoon* means to criticize, which could work, but there's no other word that also means criticize. *Abrogate* and *rescind* work in this context.

33. b) and e).

A tradition is perpetuated when the younger generation is taught how to carry it out. We're looking for words that mean something similar to *taught*. *Coach* and *instruct* are pretty straightforwardly words with that meaning. Since the sentence is vague enough, you can make a case for several other answer choices, but none have the consistency of meaning of those two.

34. a) and d).

We're looking for words that go with "even" and mean that there are no deviations. *Consistent* and *uniform* fit this meaning well and have similar meanings. *Tedious* seems like it would fit, but there's no other word that means something similar.

35. c) and f).

What would be expected if penalties for breaking the law were very harsh? Probably not breaking the law! We need words that mean "not breaking." *Quibbling, evading, defying* all indicate breaking the law, which is the opposite of what we want. *Compromising on* the law is less radically opposite, but still does not fit what we're looking for. We're left with *compliance with* and *concession to* the law.

36. c) and d).

From reading the sentence, how would you describe a characteristic that several members of a family share? "Common to" or "universal" might work. Let's examine the answer choices: *Alien, contrary,* and *atypical* are all opposites of "common to," so they should be eliminated. *Diametric* is difficult to understand in this context. However, *endemic* and *intrinsic* both mean inherent to, or universally characteristic of.

37. b).

To claim that Egyptian artists could have progressed further, the author needs to give evidence of their shortcomings as well as their potential. In this passage, she criticizes Egyptian artists for their lack of perspective and for their failure to produce individually unique work. To prove their potential, she provides evidence of the existence of poetry in Egyptian civilization. We need to find the answer choice which points to one of these planks of her argument. It is **b)**, a sentence which points out the Egyptian's crude ignorance of perspective.

38. c).

This is a common type of question found in reading comprehension passages – the ETS will select a word with many meanings from the passage and ask which meaning it takes in that particular context. In this case, *consideration* is closest to *concern* – the artist once had concern or interest, and that was telling in his story.

39. a), c), and f).

There is evidence in the passage to support the claims that Egyptian art functioned both for decoration and for the recording of history. The author also mentioned that Egyptian art was constrained by religious rules. Choice **b)** is false; the author dedicated a lot of space to explaining that the unrealistic aspects of Egyptian art, which sacrificed representation for storytelling. Choice **d)** is never mentioned in the passage. Choice **e)** is only mentioned when the author laments that Egyptian artists were not given the freedom of creative expression.

40. d).

On questions like this one, it's good to eliminate incorrect answer choices based on evidence from the text. Answer choice A is wrong because the author does make note of the existence of poetry in ancient Egypt. Answer choice B is wrong because the author's logic never rests on the assumption that depicting historical events was unimportant to Egyptian art. Choice **c)** is wrong because the author simply describes these different types of techniques; never doe she say that they were used exclusively from one another. Answer choice **e)** is wrong because the author explicitly explains this same concept in the passage. Choice **d)** is correct – the author assumes that the Egyptian style of painting without realism and perspective was crude and based in their ignorance of these techniques. If the Egyptians understood the techniques but rejected them based on a different understanding of sophistication, this argument would need to be rethought.

TEST YOUR KNOWLEDGE: QUANTITATIVE REASONING

This chapter contains 40 questions (the equivalent of two full Quantitative Reasoning sections). If you would like to time yourself, you should allot 35 minutes for each 20-question set. This mimics the form and pacing of an electronic GRE session. The question types are mixed as they would be on a GRE. The difficulty of these questions ranges from moderate to heavy. Detailed answers, along with strategy notes pertaining to the question types, are given in the next section.

For Questions 1-9, compare the two quantities given. Additional information about the two quantities may be given. Select the answer choice for each pair of quantities that best reflects their relationship. The answer choices for each of these questions are:
   a. Quantity A is greater than Quantity B.
   b. Quantity B is greater than Quantity A.
   c. The two quantities are equal.
   d. The relationship cannot be determined from the information given.

A symbol that appears throughout a question has the same meaning within the question.

The figure below will be used for questions 1 and 2.

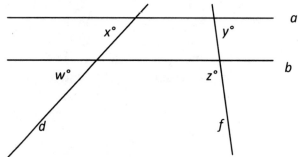

Lines a and b are parallel and intersected by lines d and f.

1.

Quantity A	Quantity B
$x^\circ + z^\circ$	$y^\circ + w^\circ$

A | B | C | D

2.

Quantity A	Quantity B
Length of line a.	Length of line b.

A | B | C | D

3. $4y < 0 < -y$.

Quantity A	Quantity B
y	$|y|$

4. $x > 0$.

Quantity A	Quantity B
$\dfrac{x+1}{x}$	$\dfrac{1}{x+1}$

Questions 5, 6, and 7 use the information in the figure below:

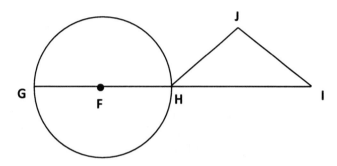

Point H lies in the middle of line GI. Triangle HIJ is an isosceles triangle, with segments HJ and IJ being equal. The length of GI is 7. Point F is the center of the circle. Angle JHI is 25°.

5.

Quantity A	Quantity B
The diameter of Circle F.	The length of HI.

6.

Quantity A	Quantity B
The area of Circle F.	3π.

7.

Quantity A	Quantity B
Angle JHI + Angle JIH.	Angle HJI.

A child went trick-or-treating and got the following haul of Halloween candy: six suckers, five chocolate fun-sized candy bars, three pieces of gum, six sour candies, and five caramels. She decides to let her brother select a candy twice at random from her bucket. Assume the probability of selecting any particular piece of candy is the same.

8.

Quantity A	Quantity B	
The probability that he will select a chocolate and then a sucker.	The probability that he will not select a piece of gum.	A B C D

The height of triangle *A* is 25% greater than the height of triangle *B*, and the base of triangle *B* is 15% longer than the base of triangle *A*.

9.

Quantity A	Quantity B	
The area of triangle *A*.	The area of triangle *B*.	A B C D

For questions 10 through 20, follow the instructions. Multiple-choice questions have only one answer, unless otherwise specified. When no choices are given and instead a grid-in box is provided, fill in the numeric entry box.

Specific instructions for numeric entry:

- Fractions do not need to be reduced unless they do not fit in the space provided.

- When a question asks for an answer in fraction form, you'll be given a fraction bar in the entry space. Otherwise, use a decimal.

- Numerically equivalent answers are treated the same. For example, 5 and 5.0.

- Use the small row to the furthest left of the box to indicate if an answer is negative.

10. What is the degree measure of the smaller angle formed by the hands of a circular wall clock that reads 2:00?
    a) 12°.
    b) 30°.
    c) 45°.
    d) 50°.
    e) 60°.

Directions: Select All Answers Which Apply:

11. If $x < 0 < y$ and $|x| > |y|$, which of the following expressions are negative?
   a) $(x + y)^2$
   b) $x^2 - y^2$
   c) xy
   d) $y^2 - x^2$
   e) $x - y$

Questions 12 and 13 Use the Following Information:

A city is planned using streets, which run north to south, and avenues, which run east to west. Avenues are intersected by streets every 50 meters, and streets are intersected by avenues every 100 meters. The street at the west edge of the city is called 1st street, and the street numbers increase as you head east. The avenue at the north edge of the city is called Avenue A, and the avenues progress alphabetically toward the south.

A person is walking from his home at the corner of 3rd Street and Avenue K to the post office at the corner of 10th street and Avenue P.

12. He walks at an average rate of 20 meters per minute without taking any detours. How many minutes does it take for him to arrive?
   Enter your answer in the boxes provided:

13. When the man arrives at the post office, how many meters is he from his home in a direct line, ignoring the buildings in the way?
   Enter your answer in the boxes provided:

Question 14 Uses the Following Figure:

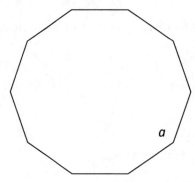

14. The polygon pictured above is a decagon: a figure with ten sides of equal length. The length of each side of this decagon is 5 units. What is the value, in degrees, of angle *a*?
   a) 36°.
   b) 100°.
   c) 136°.
   d) 144°.
   e) 200°.

Question 15 Uses the Following Data:

Study I – Crops of *Coffea arabica* grown at different elevations		
Elevation above sea level	**Crop yield – kg of beans**	**Coffee quality**
500 m	120 kg	Fair
1000 m	350 kg	Excellent
1700 m	600 kg	Good
2200 m	400 kg	Poor

Study II –*Coffea Arabica* grown at different locations and with differing caffeine contents		
Optimal elevation	**Latitude grown**	**Percent caffeine**
500 m	10° N	4%
1200 m	4° S	5%
1200 m	0° (Equatorial)	5.5%
1700 m	8° S	4%
1700 m	5° N	6%

15. A coffee corporation is looking to grow a crop of *Coffea Arabica*. They would like to maximize the crop yield and minimize the caffeine percentage of the beans. Where should they plant the crop?
   a) At 2200 meters elevation and a latitude of 5° N.
   b) At 1700 meters elevation and a latitude of 10° N.
   c) At 1200 meters elevation and a latitude of 0°.
   d) At 1700 meters elevation and a latitude of 8° S.
   e) At 1000 meters elevation and a latitude of 4° S.

Questions 16 and 17 Use the Following Information:

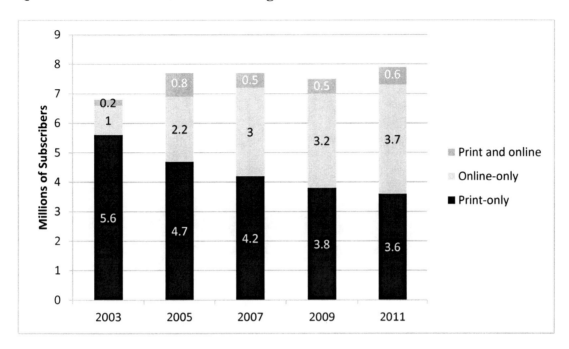

16. What was the median percentage of print subscribers who also had online access over the five-year period?
    a) 6.5%
    b) 10.6%
    c) 11.6%
    d) 14.5%
    e) 31.5%

Directions for question 17: Select All Answers that Apply:

17. In which years did total subscriptions see an increase of more than 3% from the year before?
    a) 2005
    b) 2007
    c) 2009
    d) 2011

Directions for question 18: Select All Answers that Apply:

18. Y = f(x) is graphed on a coordinate plane, where $f(x) = \frac{4 + |x|}{2}$. Which of the following pairs of (x, y) coordinates would fall below the resultant line on the plane?
    a) (-4, 2)
    b) (2, 4)
    c) (0, 3)
    d) (-2, 3)
    e) (-20, 10)

Questions 19 and 20 Use the Following Information:

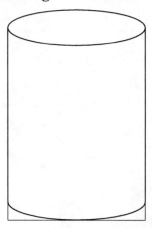

The water tower in Silver City was constructed to hold a volume of 150,000 cubic feet of water. The tower has a circular base which is centered on a square lot, as shown in the figure. The edge of the tower touches the edges of the lot at four points. The lot is 1600 square feet.

19. What the approximate height, in feet, of the water tower?
   a) 90 feet
   b) 120 feet
   c) 130 feet
   d) 150 feet
   e) 170 feet

20. During a drought, the residents of Silver City drain the previously-full water tower by 65%. How high, to the nearest foot, is the water level inside of the water tower?
   Enter your answer in the boxes provided:

If you are timing yourself, this is the end of the first 35-minute section

For Questions 21-29, compare the two quantities given. Additional information about the two quantities may be given. Select the answer choice for each pair of quantities that best reflects their relationship. The answer choices for each of these questions are:
   a. **Quantity A is greater than Quantity B.**
   b. **Quantity B is greater than Quantity A.**
   c. **The two quantities are equal.**
   d. **The relationship cannot be determined from the information given.**

21.

Quantity A	Quantity B
The number of prime factors of 84.	5.

A | B | C | D

22. $k = 67,492,048$
$j = 3,957,277$

Quantity A	Quantity B
The units digit of kj.	The tens digit of kj.

A | B | C | D

Questions 23 and 24 Use the Following Information:

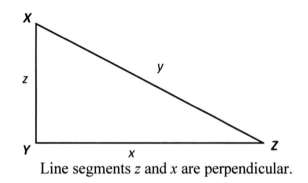

Line segments z and x are perpendicular.

23.

Quantity A	Quantity B
Angle X.	Angle Z.

A | B | C | D

24.

Quantity A	Quantity B
Angle X + Angle Z.	Angle Y.

A | B | C | D

131

On setting 1, a printer prints 80 pages in three minutes. On setting 2, the same printer prints 100 pages in four minutes.

25.

Quantity A	Quantity B		A	B	C	D

Pages printed on setting 1 in ten minutes.

Pages printed on setting 2 in ten minutes.

City administrators estimate that between 25% and 35% of city residents subscribe to the local cable access channel. The cable access channel has 45,300 local subscribers.

26.

Quantity A	Quantity B		A	B	C	D

178,000

The city's population

There are four numbers in a set. The largest number is four times the smallest number. The difference between the two middle numbers is 8. The mode of the set is 9. The mean of the set is 17.75.

27.

Quantity A	Quantity B		A	B	C	D

The range of the set.

The third number in the set.

28.

Quantity A	Quantity B		A	B	C	D

45.

The sum of all multiples of 7 between 15 and 30.

Question 29 Uses the Following Information:

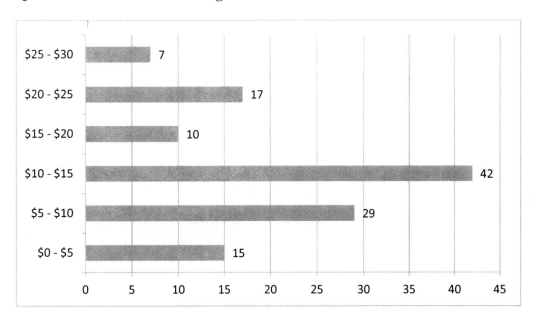

The management at an arcade aggregated per-customer spending on a Saturday evening. Above is the distribution chart of the spending levels of customers that night.

29.

Quantity A	Quantity B
The minimum possible sales made that night.	The maximum possible sales made at the most common spending level.

A	B	C	D

Questions 30 and 31 Use the Following Information:

Three intersecting lines enclose a figure on the coordinate plane. The equations of the lines are:

$$y = 4$$
$$-2y = x + 4$$
$$x = 1$$

30. What is the approximate area of the figure enclosed by these lines, in units squared?
   a) 28.
   b) 34.
   c) 38.
   d) 42.
   e) 46.

31. What is the approximate length of the longest side of the figure?
   a) 6.50 units.
   b) 13.00 units.
   c) 14.53 units.
   d) 70.21 units.
   e) 211.25 units.

Directions: Select all that apply:

32. Function $f(x)$ is defined for all integers where:

$$f(x) = 2x + 4 \qquad \text{if } x > 40$$
$$f(x) = x^2 \qquad \text{if } x \leq 40$$

Which of the following numbers can be values of $f(x)$ for both values of x that are greater than 40 and values of x that are less than or equal to 40? Select all correct answers.
   a) 0.
   b) 64.
   c) 121.
   d) 225.
   e) 900.
   f) 1444.

The following information is used in questions 33 and 34:

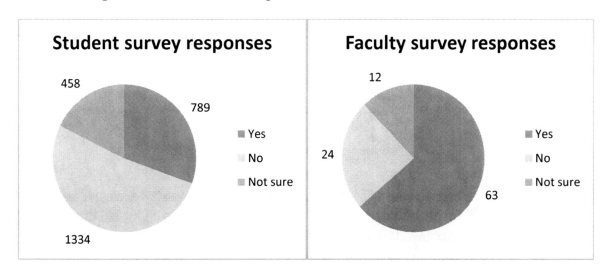

Students and faculty at a small college were surveyed by the administration to determine whether they would find it useful to have a college-affiliated email account provided to them.

33. What is the approximate aggregated total percentage of those surveyed who would not find a college-affiliated email address useful?
    a) 25%.
    b) 35%.
    c) 50%.
    d) 65%.
    e) 75%.

34. Approximately how much greater is the percentage of faculty who would find the email address useful than the percentage of students who would find it useful?
    a) 50%.
    b) 100%.
    c) 200%.
    d) 300%.
    e) 400%.

Directions: select all that apply:

35. A four-digit number is divided by 6. The remainder of the division is 2. Which of the following could possibly be the last digit of the four-digit number?
    a) 1.
    b) 2.
    c) 3.
    d) 4.
    e) 5.
    f) 6.

36. There are twenty different organic chemistry labs offered at a college. A lab happens either on Mondays or on Thursdays. 50% of the labs are offered in the morning, and 30% of the labs happen on Thursdays. If six labs are scheduled for Monday morning, how many labs are scheduled for Monday afternoon?

Enter your answer in the boxes provided:

37. Rolling a die in a board game will result in 3 different and mutually exclusive scenarios for the player. The probabilities of each of these scenarios occurring, respectively, are p, $\frac{p}{3}$, and $2p$. What is the probability of the least likely scenario occurring?

Enter your answer in the boxes provided in the form of a fraction:

Questions 38 and 39 Use the Following Information:

The lockers for rent at a waterpark have locks that open when a specific string of digits is entered. Each lock is programmed to open at a different 3-digit string, ranging from 000 to 999.

38. Eleanor forgot the code to open her rented locker, but she remembers that two of the digits are 5 and 7. How many different possible combinations could open the locker?

Enter your answer in the boxes provided:

39. The waterpark currently has 200 lockers available for rent. How many more lockers must be added before it is necessary to switch to 4-digit codes, assuming that every locker must have a unique code?

Enter your answer in the boxes provided:

40. A sprocket manufacturer has determined that the demand for sprockets changes linearly at different price points. When sprockets were priced at $1.27 apiece, the manufacturer sold 45,000 of them in a month. When they were priced at $2.41, 38,000 were sold in a month. This month, the manufacturer anticipated producing 42,500 sprockets. How should they be priced to ensure that each one is sold without a shortage? Round your answer to the nearest penny.

Enter your answer in the boxes provided:

TEST YOUR KNOWLEDGE: QUANTITATIVE REASONING—ANSWERS

1. **c).**
   The two quantities are equal. Because lines *a* and *b* are parallel, we can apply the properties of corresponding angles to the angles created by the intersecting lines. *X* and *W* are equal angles. Any time two lines intersect, the angles formed opposite of one another will be equal, and any two angles next to one another will add up to 90°. So, the angle opposite of *X* is equal to it, and *W* corresponds (holds the same position as on a different parallel line) to this angle, so *X* and *W* are equal angles. The same is true, by the same reasoning, for angles *Y* and *Z*. Therefore, adding *X* and *Z* together is the same as adding *W* and *Y* together.

2. **d).**
   The relationship cannot be determined by the given information. We are told nothing about the lengths of these lines; we can't infer anything about length just by knowing that they are parallel.

3. **b).**
   Quantity B is greater. We can tell from the given information that *y* must be negative, so the absolute value of *y* will be greater because it will be positive. Remember, absolute value means the distance of the integer from 0 on the number line. It is never negative.

4. **a).**
   Quantity A is greater. Since we know that *x* can be any positive number, we need to test the formulas in both columns with different numbers, including a fraction, to see if there's a relationship that holds the same or if it can't be determined. Let's use a chart to plug in different values for *x*:

If *x* = ?	Quantity A	Quantity B
1	(1+1)/1 = 2	1/(1+1) = 1/2
1/2	(.5+1)/.5 = 3	1/(1+.5) = 2/3
100	(100+1)/100 = 1.01	1/(100+1) = .009

   It looks like Quantity A is always greater!

5. **c).**
   The two quantities are equal. The first thing you'll want to do is copy the figure down on your scratch paper and label what you know: *H* bisects *GI*, so *GH* is the same length as *HI*. *HIJ* is isosceles, so you should mark *HJ* and *IJ* as equal lengths. Then, since we know that *GI*'s length is 7, you can mark that as well. You can also label *GHI*. There are some additional notes you can make, given this information. For example, *JIH* is also 25°, since the triangle is isosceles. Once you've labeled this, you already have the answer to question 5; the circle's diameter is line segment *GH*, which is equal to *HI*.

6. **a).**

Quantity A is greater. The formula for the area of a circle is $A = \pi r^2$. The radius is segment FH (or GF, or F to any point on the circumference). We know that GH is 3.5 in length, because it is one half of the line GI, which is given as 7 in length. FH is one half of GH, so it's 1.75 long (we know this because F is in the center of the circle, halfway between G and H). So, the area of Circle F is $\pi(1.75)^2$. This is equal to 3.0625π (here is where you'd want to use that calculator. It doesn't have a square button, so you just have to multiply 1.75 * 1.75). This is bigger than 3π.

7. **b).**

Quantity B is greater. We know that angle JHI is 25°. Therefore, angle JIH must also be 25°, because this is an isosceles triangle with segments HJ and IJ being equal. Remember, in an isosceles triangle, two angles are equal. The odd angle out is the one where the equal line segments meet; in this case, that's angle HJI. Therefore, angle JHI + angle JIH = 25° + 25° = 50°. How do we know the size of angle HJI? It must be all the leftover degrees in the triangle. Therefore, angle HJI = 180°– 50° = 130°.

8. **b).**

Quantity B is greater. This is a compound event probability problem. To calculate Quantity A, we must multiply the probability that he first selects a chocolate by the probability that he then selects a sucker. That looks like this:

$$\frac{5 * 6}{25 * 24}$$

5/25 is the probability of first selecting a chocolate, and 6/24 is the probability of then selecting a sucker (since only 24 candies are left in the bucket after he takes the first. We don't need to multiply this out; just writing the expression is enough for this step. To calculate Quantity B, we need to multiply the probability that he will *not* choose a piece of gum by the probability that he will also *not* choose a piece of gum on his second draw. That looks like this:

$$\frac{22 * 21}{25 * 24}$$

The denominator is the same. There are 22 non-gum candies in the bucket, so the probability that he will choose one of those first is 22/25. For his second draw, there are 21 non-gum candies in the bucket, which now has 24 candies total.

You don't even need to do the arithmetic to see the 22 * 21 will be greater than 5 * 6, and since the denominators are the same, that's enough to answer the problem.

9. a).

The area of Triangle A is greater. The formula for the area of a triangle is $a = (1/2)bh$, where b is the base of the triangle and h is the height. It doesn't matter which side of the triangle is chosen as the base; and the height of a triangle is the perpendicular line from the base to opposite angle. For example:

In this triangle, the bottom leg is the base, and the dotted line is the height.

To solve this problem, we have two options. We can answer algebraically, or we can plug in numbers. If we plug in numbers, we need to make sure that we're solving the problem universally, so we may have to do it more than once.

Algebraic method:
Let's say that B is the base of Triangle A, and H is the height of triangle B. We organized it like that because it's easier to call the smaller base B, and then call the larger base (1.15) B. So:

Area of Triangle $A = (0.5)(1.25H)(B) = .625BH$
Area of Triangle $B = (0.5)(H)(1.15B) = .575BH$

Plug-in method:
If you don't like to represent things algebraically, then you can plug in on this problem. Plugging in is risky in general, because you may be making false assumptions, but when you're dealing with percentages it's more likely to work. Also, dealing with geometric figures precludes negative values, so that helps too.

It's still easiest to assign numbers to the smaller values first, since the given percentages are increases. So let's say that Triangle A has a base of 100, and Triangle B has a height of 100. This means the height of A will be 125, and the base of B will be 115. So our formulas are:

Area of $A = .5 (100) (125)$
Area of $B = .5 (115) (100)$

We can see that A will be bigger. We should double-check that this holds true when we change up the numbers. For example, since A has the greater height, let's make height really small and see what happens. Height of $A = 5$, height of $B = 4$. 5 is 25% greater than 4.

Area of $A = .5 (100) (5)$
Area of $B = .5 (115) (4)$

Nope, A is still bigger. Also, the algebraic method is faster, so consider practicing that way so that you can use your time efficiently during the test.

10. e).

A clock has twelve segments, and the angle formed by the hands at 2:00 will include two of those segments. Therefore we can use a proportion:

$$\frac{x}{360} = \frac{2}{12}$$

To solve, multiply 2/12 by 360. The answer is 60°.

11. c), d), and e).

We know that x is negative, y is positive, and that the absolute value of x is greater than the absolute value of y (x is a "bigger" negative number than y is a positive number, like -40 and 4, for example). So, which of the expressions can be negative?

    a. $(x + y)^2$

       No, because the whole expression is squared, which makes it positive.

    b. $x^2 - y^2$

       No, x^2 will be bigger than y^2, so this will be positive,

    c. xy

       Yes, because a negative number times a positive number is negative.

    d. $y^2 - x^2$

       Yes, because y^2 will be smaller than x^2, so subtracting x^2 yields a negative

    e. $x - y$

       Yes; a negative number minus a positive number is negative.

You can substitute in two numbers that fit the criteria if you want, but moving through the choices in the abstract is faster for this question.

12. 42.5 minutes.

Here is another problem for which it is best to begin by drawing:

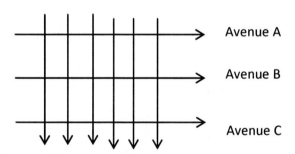

So, we have these streets and avenues. The avenues run down your page and are labeled A, B, C; and the streets run across the page and should be labeled 1, 2, 3. Streets are closer together than avenues: they occur every 50 meters, and the avenues are every 100 meters. Drawing this out helps you visualize the situation and understand how to handle the next step. It's not necessary to draw out all the streets mentioned and then count the blocks; we can do that part algebraically.

So for problem 12, we know this man is walking from 3rd and K to 10th and P. How many street blocks is he crossing? 7. How many avenue blocks is he crossing? 5. So his total distance traveled will be (50 * 7) + (100 * 5) = 850 meters.

Careful! The question isn't asking you how many meters he walks; it's asking you how many minutes it will take him. He walks at a rate of 20 meters per minute. Rate problems can be solved with the equation Distance = Rate * Time. The important thing to remember with these problems is that your rate needs to be given in the same units as your distance and your time. In this case, everything is given in meters and minutes, so we don't need to worry about converting anything. So, 850 = 20 * T. We solve for T, time, by dividing 850 by 20. It will take him 42.5 minutes to walk to the post office.

13. 610.32 meters.

This problem uses the same information and map as above, so we've already done some of the work! Now we want to know the linear distance between the post office and his house. This is a Pythagorean triangle problem, because the streets and avenues occur at right angles to one another, forming the sides of a right triangle. We know that he is 7 street-distance blocks and 5 avenue-distance blocks away from his house. Let's draw the triangle:

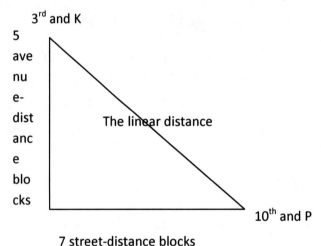

We're trying to find the hypotenuse: the long line. First, we need to convert everything to meters, because we can't work with blocks of different lengths. The height is six 100-meter blocks, or 500 meters. The length is seven 50-meter blocks, or 350 meters.

The formula for the lengths of the sides of a right triangle is: $a^2 + b^2 = c^2$, where a and b are the shorter sides and c is the hypotenuse. So we can plug in our meter distances:

$$500^2 + 350^2 = c^2$$

Then solve:
$$250000 + 122500 = c^2$$
$$372500 = c^2$$
$$610.32 = c$$

14. d).

This problem requires you to either memorize the size of the interior angles of a decagon or, even better, the formula to figure it out. The formula to find the sum of the interior angles of any polygon looks like this:

$$(n-2) * 180°$$

Where n is the number of sides the polygon has. You can remember this formula by thinking about a triangle, which you know has 180° total in its three angles. Three sides minus two is one. 1 * 180 is 180°. This simplest case can help to trigger your memory.

To find the number of degrees in each individual angle, you just divide the above formula by n, the number of sides (which is the same as the number of angles). Let's see what that looks like for a decagon:

$$\frac{(n-2) * 180}{n}$$

$$\frac{(10-2) * 180}{10}$$

When you solve this expression, it works out to 144°.

If you don't know the formula, try this method: divide the figure into equilateral triangles, and then count the number of 60° angles which fit into the interior angles of the decagon.

However, if that kind of reasoning doesn't come naturally, you should memorize the formula. Do not spend several minutes trying to reason out a problem like this if you don't know the formula, unless you've answered all the other problems in the section.

15. d).

We have to use both tables to find the correct answer. We want to maximize the crop yield – that indicates the crop grown at 1700 meters in Study I. Study II shows the caffeine percentages of crops grown at different elevations and latitudes. There are two crops in Study II that were grown at 1700 meters; the one planted at latitude 8° S has a lower caffeine percentage.

16. c).

To calculate this, we need to find the percentage of print subscribers who also have an online subscription for each year. Then we can put those percentages into increasing numerical order to find the median (the one in the middle). To find this percentage for each year, divide the number of "online and print" subscribers by the number of subscribers with both online and print and print-only subscriptions. The fractions for each year will have the numerator (top portion of the bar) divided by the denominator (numerator plus the number in the bottom portion of the bar). We don't have to worry about converting them to millions of subscribers, since we are looking for percentages. For example, in 2003, there were .2 million online and print subscribers and 5.6 print-only subscribers, so to find the percentage we'll set up the fraction: $\frac{.2}{(.2+5.6)}$.

When we divide this out, we get .034, or 3.4%. If we do this for each year, we get percentages of: 3.4%, 14.5%, 10.6%, 11.6%, and 14.3%. The one with the median (middle) value is 11.6%, which happened to be in 2009.

17. a).

This question is asking which years saw a 3% or more *increase* in subscriptions from the year before. We can eliminate 2009 just by looking at the graph, because total subscriptions went down in that year. To find the total subscriptions for each year, we just add up the three portions of the bar representing subscriptions for that year. You can also estimate the total for each year by looking at the vertical axis. To find if subscriptions went up by at least 3% in a year, take the total for the year before and multiply it by 1.03. If the resultant number is lower than the total subscriptions in the next year, then they went up by more than 3%. For example, to see if subscriptions in 2005 are greater than those in 2003 by more than 3%, we do the following:

Add the three subscription types for 2005 to find total subscriptions:
$5.6 + 1 + 0.2 = 6.8$

Multiply this number by 1.03 to get our baseline for growth:
$6.8 \times 1.03 = 7.004$

Were total subscriptions in 2005 greater than 7.0 million? Yes, the bar on the graph is well above the 7.0 line.

Going through this process for the other years, or estimating based on the graph, reveals that 2005 is the only year for which subscriptions grew by more than 3% from the year before.

18. a) and e).

You can sketch this graph out if you want to, but it's not necessary for solving the problem.

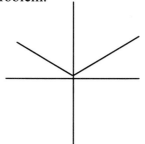

If you do sketch it, the graph will look like the figure at right – absolute value graphs always reflect about an axis. If the graph takes the absolute value of *y*, it will reflect about the x-axis. If it takes the absolute value of *x*, as this one does, it will reflect about the y-axis.

Let's rewrite the equation to make it simpler:

$$y = 2 + \frac{|x|}{2}$$

What does it mean for a point to fall "below" a line? Looking at the graph, we can see that for a point to fall below the line, it has to have a *y* value less than the *y* value at that coordinate. So, let's test the coordinates given in each answer choice:

(-4, 2) What should *y* equal if we plug in -4 for *x*? $2 + \frac{|-4|}{2} = 4$. Will this point be below the line? Yes, because when x = -4, the line is at y = 4. 2.

(2, 4) Where will the line be when *x* = 2? When we plug 2 into our equation, we get *y* = 3. Is this point below the line? No, 4 is bigger than 3.

(0, 3) When *x* = 0, the line will be at *y* = 2. This point is above the line.

(-2, 3) When *x* = -2, the line will be at 3. This point is *on* the line, not above or below it. We can't select this point, because we're only looking for points that fall below the line.

(-20, 10) When *x* = -20, where is the line? At $y = 2 + \frac{|-20|}{2} = 12$. This point is below the line.

19. b).

This is a "volume of a solid" problem. What shape is our solid? It is a cylinder. The formula for the volume of a cylinder is: $V = \pi r^2 *$ height.

What information do we have? We know that the volume is 150,000 cubic feet. We know that the diameter of the circular base is the same length as the side of the square lot.

The square lot has an area of 1600 square feet. What is the length of one side? $\sqrt{1600} = 40$.

Okay, if our diameter is 40 feet, then our radius is half of that: 20 feet. Therefore, we can find the height by using our volume formula, and using 3.14 for the value of pi:
$V = \pi r^2 *$ height

$$150000 = \pi(20)^2 *\text{ height}$$
$$150000 = 1256 *\text{ height}$$
$$119.4 = \text{height}$$

This then rounds to 120 feet, which is answer choice **b)**.

20. 77 feet.

Careful – the *volume* is what was drained by 65%, not the height (or, water level). First, let's solve to see what the volume of water inside the tower is now:

Original volume: 150,000
65% of 150,000 = (150,000) * .65 = 97,500 feet (this is where the 97,500 should be subtracted from the original volume to find the remaining volume after 65% has been removed. If the question had said that the water towers volume had been reduced *to* 65% of its original volume, the remaining volume would reflect 65%.

Okay! Now that we have the new volume, we can find the new water level height, using the same steps as in the problem above. Remember, the radius hasn't changed:

$$150000 - 97500 = 52500 = \pi(20)^2 *\text{ height}$$
$$52500 = 1256 *\text{ height}$$
$$41.7 = \text{height}$$

This is a great bonus of writing out your work. One side of the equation did not even change! Notice that the instructions tell you to round to the nearest foot, so you should grid in 42.

21. b).

Quantity B is greater than Quantity A, as 84 has only 4 prime numbers (counting the 2s separately). For choice **c)** to be correct, and the quantities equal, then the number 5 for Quantity B would need to be changed to 4. To find the prime factors of a number, simply reduce until you can't anymore. For example:

84 = 2 * 42	84 = 2 * 42
84 = 2 * 2 * 21	84 = 2 * 7 * 6
84 = 2 * 2 * 3 * 7	84 = 2 * 7 * 3 * 2

84 has 4 prime factors. Remember, 1 is not considered a prime number. A prime number is any number that has *two* factors: 1 and itself. For example, 2 = 1 * 2, so two is prime because those are the only positive whole number factors that you can multiply to get 2.

22. a).

This question is written to confuse you into doing unnecessary computations. You are being asked to compare two digits in the product of two very large numbers. Which digit of the product is higher, the tens digit or the units (ones) digit? Since these are the last two digits of the product, it is not necessary to compute the entire product. If you input the whole multiplication into your calculator, you're likely to make a mistake.

Instead of multiplying out 67,492,048 and 3,957,277, we can take the tens and units digits of those numbers – 48 and 77 – and multiply those. This is much simpler to input on a calculator, and you will get 3696 as the product. Even better, if you're doing this by hand, you only need to multiply far enough to find the tens and units digits of the product – 96.

Once we know that the tens and units digits of the product of those numbers is 96, then it is clear that the tens digit – 9 – is larger than the units digit – 6.

23. d).

We know that Angle Y must be 90°, since the lines that form it are perpendicular, but beyond that, we don't have enough information about the size of other angles.

24. c).

Since Angle Y is 90°, the other two angles must also add up to 90°. Remember, the three angles of a triangle must always total 180°.

25. a).

This is a rates problem. With rates like this, you can set up a proportion to find the value of each quantity. Let's look at Quantity A:

$$\frac{80 \; pages}{3 \; minutes} = \frac{x \; pages}{10 \; minutes}$$

The key to setting up this proportion is to keep the units in the corresponding places in each fraction: number of pages over number of minutes. It works the other way around as well, if you prefer.

When we solve this algebraically, we see that setting 1 produces 266.6 pages in ten minutes.

Quantity B: We'll set this proportion up in the same way.

$$\frac{100 \; pages}{4 \; minutes} = \frac{x \; pages}{10 \; minutes}$$

When we solve this proportion, we see that setting 2 will print 250 pages in 10 minutes.

Over the course of 10 minutes, setting 1 is more prolific.

Another way to solve this problem is to simply reduce the rate of each setting. The one with the faster rate will produce more copies in 10 minutes. This only works because we're being asked to solve both quantities for the same timeframe; if the question asked us to compare the output of setting 1 in 5 minutes with the output of setting 2 in 7 minutes, we'd have to solve each one individually.

To compare the rates, we just need to get each rate in a fraction with the same denominator.

Setting 1: $\frac{80\ pages}{3\ minutes} = \frac{80}{3} = \frac{26.6}{1}$

Setting 2: $\frac{100\ pages}{4\ minutes} = \frac{100}{4} = \frac{25}{1}$

Once we reduce each rate to pages per minute, we see that setting 1 is slightly faster.

26. d).

From the information given, we can determine a possible range of the city's population. If 25% of the residents subscribe to the cable channel, then the population can be expressed as:

(Population) * .25 = 45,300.   Solving this gives us a population of 181,000.

However, if 35% of the population subscribes, then we set up the problem like this:

(Population) * .35 = 45,300.   Solving this gives us a population of 129,428.

Quantity A is between these two numbers, within the range of the city's possible populations, based on the given information. Therefore, we don't have enough information to determine whether the population is greater than that number.

You may have only needed to work out the first step to see this, but when the numbers are a little closer, or you are unsure, or if you have extra time, it's always a good idea to work out both ends of the range before answering a question like this.

27. a).

To solve this problem, we just need to work through each piece of given information. We have four numbers:

$$\_\_\_,\ \_\_\_,\ \_\_\_,\ \_\_\_\_$$

We know that the biggest number is four times the smallest number:

$$x,\ \_\_\_,\ \_\_\_,\ 4x$$

We know that the difference between the two middle numbers is 8:

$$x, y, y + 8, 4x$$

We know that the mode of the set is 9, meaning that at least two of the numbers equal 9. But the directions also allow us to know that only two, no more, of the numbers equal 9.

The mean of the set is 17.75.

Let's do an experiment: say that x and y are both 9. That means our set looks like this:

$$9, 9, 17, 36.$$

Is the mean of this set 17.75?

$$\frac{9+9+17+36}{4} = 17.75$$

Yes it is! We've confirmed our set. Now we need to find Quantities A and B.
Quantity A: The range of the set. Remember that range means the difference between the highest and lowest numbers of the set. Our range is $36 - 9 = 27$.

Quantity B: The third number in the set. That is 17. Quantity A is larger.

28. b).

This one looks weird, but is very easy. What is the sum of all the multiples of 7 between 15 and 30? The only multiples of 7 within that range are 21 and 28.

$$21 + 28 = 49$$

49 (Quantity B) is greater than 45 (Quantity A).

29. a).

This is a frequency distribution graph. You'll probably see one on your test – the GRE likes these! A frequency distribution graph organizes data by the number of observations at each level. For example, a distribution graph showing average rainfall by state might say that 3 states have an average rainfall of less than 5 inches, 7 states have an average rainfall between 5 and 10 inches, etc.

This distribution graph shows how many customers spent each level of money at the arcade in one night. We are asked to compare the minimum possible total sales with the maximum total sales possible in one category.

Quantity A: To find the minimum possible sales, we simply add up the low-end totals for each category. For example, we know that 15 customers spent between $0 - $5. We'll assume they all spent $0. For the next category, we have 29 customers spending $5, which gives us $145. Do this for each column, using the low estimate of the spending level, and you get $1230 total.

Quantity B: To find the maximum possible sales made at the most-common spending level, we multiply the number of customers who spent at that level by that level's high-end estimate. We can see from the graph that the most common spending level was $10 - $15, and that 42 people spent within that level. So the maximum possible value would be 42 * 15 = 630, which is definitely lower than Quantity A.

30. d).

The first thing you should do with this problem is change the formula of that second line, because it's just awful!

$$-2y = x + 4$$
$$y = -\frac{1}{2}x - 2$$

Much better! Next, sketch a graph of the three lines (unless you already "get" the problem and know what to do).

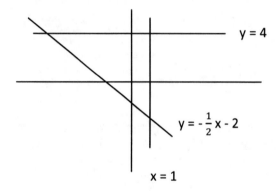

Now we can see that we have a triangle framed by these three lines. And look! One of our lines is parallel with the x-axis, and one is parallel with the y-axis, making them perpendicular to each other. It's a right triangle!

How do we find the area of a right triangle?

$$\text{Area} = \frac{1}{2}(\text{base}) * (\text{height})$$

The base and height are the lengths of the shorter two legs (not the hypotenuse).

We need to find the lengths of the line segments making up the legs. The best way to do this is to find the points at the three corners of the triangle, and then calculate the distance between those points.

We know that x = 1 and y = 4 intersect at (1, 4).

150

To find where $x = 1$ and $y = -\frac{1}{2}x - 2$ intersect, we plug x = 1 into the line:

$$y = -\frac{1}{2}(1) - 2$$
$$y = -\frac{1}{2} - 2$$
$$y = -\frac{5}{2}$$

They intersect at $(1, -\frac{5}{2})$.

We do the same step to find where $y = 4$ and $y = -\frac{1}{2}x - 2$ intersect:

$$4 = -\frac{1}{2}x - 2$$
$$6 = -\frac{1}{2}x$$
$$-12 = x$$

They intersect at (-12, 4).

Now we label our points on the graph:

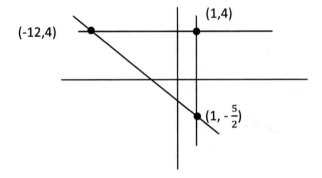

Great! Now, find the length of the base and the height by counting along the lines. The segment parallel to the x-axis is 13 units long, from -12 to 1. The line parallel to the y-axis is 6.5 long, from 4 to $-\frac{5}{2}$. We can plug these lengths into our area formula:

$$\text{Area} = \frac{1}{2}(13) * (6.5)$$
$$\text{Area} = 42.25 \text{ units squared}$$

31. c).

This question makes use of all the work we did for the problem above. What is the length of the longest side of the figure? Since we have a right triangle, we know that the longest side is a hypotenuse. There are two ways to solve this problem: the Pythagorean theorem, or the distance formula.

151

Pythagorean Theorem:
We simply take the lengths of the two short sides to find the length of the hypotenuse.

Use this formula:

$$a^2 + b^2 = c^2$$

a and *b* are the shorter sides, and *c* is the hypotenuse.

$$13^2 + 6.5^2 = c^2$$
$$169 + 42.25 = c^2$$

$$211.25 = c^2$$
$$14.53 = c$$

You can also approach this problem using the distance formula, but you'll quickly realize that you're doing the exact same thing, because the distance formula is based on treating two points as the corners of a right triangle!

The formula for the distance between two points is:

$$\text{distance}^2 = (\text{distance between } x \text{ coordinates})^2 + (\text{distance between } y \text{ coordinates})^2$$

Does that look familiar? We can plug in the *x* and *y* coordinates for the two points at the end of the hypotenuse:

$$\text{distance}^2 = (1 - -12\,)^2 + (4 - -\frac{5}{2}\,)^2$$
$$\text{distance}^2 = (13)^2 + (6.5)^2$$

From here, you find the answer is 14.53 units.

32. e) and f).

A function is just a set of instructions about what to do with a number to get another number. For example: the equation of a line tells us how to interpret *y* coordinates, given the *x* coordinates in a set.

This function has a twist: you choose the operation to perform depending on the size of your input, or *x*, value.

The question ask us to identify values which are possible results, or *y*-values, of *f(x)* for inputs less than 40, and greater than 40, or equal to 40.

It's tempting to work backwards from the answer choices, but that doesn't really work – you may be put in the position of working out ten equations that way. If you have lots of time, then this could be an option, but it's better to approach the problem strategically.

When faced with a problem like this, it is helpful to understand the most extreme cases. In this instance, extreme cases for the value of x would include 40 and 41, to see the highest possible value for $x \leq 40$ and the lowest possible value for $x > 40$. This will give us an idea of the overlap of the two functions.

$$f(x) = 2x + 4 \quad \text{if } x > 40.$$
$$f(x) = x^2 \qquad \text{if } x \leq 40.$$

If $x = 41$, then $f(x) = 2(41) + 4$.
If $x = 40$, then $f(x) = 86$.

If $x = 40$, then $f(x) = 40^2$.
If $x = 40$, then $f(x) = 1600$.

Now we know that one function can have results no higher than 1600 and the other can have results no lower than 86. Any values outside those bounds have to be eliminated, because it is impossible for both functions to have that result. This gets rid of answer choices **a)** and **b)**.

Another thing to notice about the functions is that the second one, $f(x) = x^2$, can only result in values that are perfect squares. This doesn't help us eliminate anything for this problem because all the answer choices do have even square roots, but it may have been useful, so remember to watch out for things like that.

What will all results of the first function, $f(x) = 2x + 4$, have in common? They will be even. Any number multiplied by two will be even:
$$1 * 2 = 2$$
$$5 * 2 = 10$$
$$121 * 2 = 242$$

Adding four to the result still keeps the answer an even number. Noticing this helps us to eliminate answer choices **c)** and **d)** as impossible. We are left with answer choices **e)** and **f)**. If you have time, you can find the numbers that satisfying the restraints of the two functions and get those results:

$$900 = 2x + 4$$
$x = 448$, which is greater than 40.

$$900 = x^2$$
$30 = x$, which is less than 40.

$$1444 = 2x + 4$$
$x = 720$, which is greater than 40.

$$1444 = x^2$$

$38 = x$, which is less than 40.

Those work! You don't *have* to test them after considering the different equations, but if you have the time, it's nice to check your work.

33. c).

To find the aggregated percentage of "no's" we need to add up the total number of both students and faculty members who voted no. We also need to add up the total number of respondents for both student and faculty, as that will be our denominator for this percentage.

Notice that the problem says "approximate percentage." That means we don't have to be too finicky in our addition; we can round things up and down:

$$\frac{total\ number\ of\ "no's"}{total\ number\ of\ respondents} = \text{aggregate total percentage of "no's"}$$

$$\frac{1330+25}{460+780+1330+65+25+10} = \text{aggregate total percentage of "no's"}$$

Notice that we rounded all the numbers. If you're comfortable with mental math, this is where you should practice it. For example, you can mentally estimate the total number of student responses to be 2600 and the total number of faculty responses to be 100.

$$\frac{1355}{2670} = \text{aggregate total percentage of "no's"}$$

Total percentage: approximately 50%

It's a little different to estimate just from the answer choices, since the percentages among the students voting no and the faculty members voting no is so different. However, if you recognize that the sheer size of the student body overwhelms the faculty size, you might feel comfortable picking **c)** just by looking at the graphs. Any time a question urges you to approximate, this kind of shoot-from-the-hip response is appropriate so long as you feel comfortable.

34. b).

How much greater is the percent of faculty who would find the email address useful than the percentage of students who would? First, let's estimate some numbers. It looks like somewhere between one-fourth and one-third of students said they would find the address useful, and something like two-thirds of faculty said that they would. Therefore, the percentage of faculty members who said yes is about twice the percentage of students who said yes. This is a question that you can answer entirely visually, once you understand what's being asked.

"Twice" is the same as "100% greater" (consider that 4 is 100% greater than 2).

35. a), b), c), d), and e).

This is one of those strange numeric reasoning problems which are solely within the purview of standardized tests.

Since it is a "select all that apply" question, we know that we can select an answer if we can think of at least one case where it is true.

The first couple of digits of the number don't matter because we can assume that they are evenly divisible by 6; only the last two will affect the remainder (the whole integers left over when you divide a number by another number).

Let's consider each answer choice:

a)	1	What two-digit number would give a remainder of 1? How about 67: 6 would divide evenly into the 66, leaving over 1. We can select this option.
b)	2	Can we think of a two-digit number that would give a remainder of 2? 68 works.
c)	3	69 would leave a remainder of 3.
d)	4	70 would leave a remainder of 4.
e)	5	71 would leave a remainder of 5.
f)	6	72 would leave – oh wait. 72 is evenly divisible by 6. Is it possible to have a remainder of six? No.

36. 8.

This is a probability problem.

We have 20 total labs. 30% of them, or 6 labs, happen on Thursdays.

50% of them, or 10 labs, happen in the morning.

We know that 6 labs happen on Monday morning. What does that tell us?

- Since only 6 labs happen on Thursday, that means that 14 labs are held on Monday.

- If 6 labs happen Monday morning, then 8 must be held in the afternoon.

By simply reasoning through the information given, we see that the answer must be 8.

37. $\frac{3}{30}$ **or** $\frac{1}{10}$.

Here's a slightly more complicated problem dealing with probabilities. What do we know?

There are three different, mutually exclusive, outcomes. This means that we can't have two outcomes happening simultaneously. This also tells us that the probability of all three outcomes must add up to 1: if there are three possible results, and only three results, they must account for the universe of possibilities: 100%, or 1.

So, we can set up the probabilities into this equation:

$$p + \frac{p}{3} + 2p = 1$$

$$\frac{p}{3} + 3p = 1$$

$$\frac{p}{3} + \frac{3p}{1} = 1$$

$$\frac{p}{3} + \frac{9p}{3} = 1$$

$$\frac{10p}{3} = 1$$
$$10p = 3$$
$$p = \frac{3}{10}$$

A little nasty, but not too bad! Since your answer must be given as a fraction, it's best to keep working in fractions. Now, for the real question: what is the probability of the least likely scenario occurring?

Which is the least likely: $\frac{3}{10}$, $\frac{3}{10(3)}$, or $\frac{6}{10}$?

That would be $\frac{3}{10(3)}$, which is $\frac{3}{30}$, or $\frac{1}{10}$.

Both of these fractions, $\frac{3}{30}$ and $\frac{1}{10}$, are equivalent, and they would both be considered right.

38. 60.

Here we have a combination/permutation problem! But which is it?

This must be a permutation problem, because order matters.

We know that the code contains a 5, a 7, and one other digit between 0 and 9.

Where could the 5 go? There are three possibilities: the first, second, or third digit.

Where could the 7 go? There are two possibilities: either of the digits not taken up by the five.

This leaves one open slot. There are ten possibilities for this slot: a 0, a 1, a 2, etc. Therefore, the number of possible codes we have is:

$$3 * 2 * 10 = 60$$

Three possibilities for one known digit to be placed in the code, two possibilities for the other known digit to be placed, and 10 possibilities of what the remaining digit can be.

39. 800.

To solve this problem, we need to know how many possible unique codes exist within the three-digit framework. How do we find this out? This is also a permutation problem, so we consider the possibilities:

$$10 * 10 * 10 = 1,000.$$

We can set the problem up this way because we know that digits can repeat within a code; for example, 000 is a valid code. Therefore, the number of possible codes is 10 (possibilities for digit one) times 10 (possibilities for digit 2) times 10 (possibilities for digit three).

However, we are not done: the question asks how many more lockers have to be built before this code system is not adequate. We currently have 200 lockers, so the park can add 800 more lockers and still assign each one a unique code. Once they have built the 1,001st locker, however, four-digit codes are needed.

40. $1.68.

This is an algebraic problem requiring us to develop a formula. We can treat the given facts as two points: when the price (x) is $1.27, the demand (y) is 45,000. When the price (x) is $2.41, the demand (y) is 38,000. To develop an equation expressing the linear relationship between these two points, we first find the slope:

$$\frac{difference\ in\ y\ coordinates}{difference\ in\ x\ coordinates} = \text{slope}$$
$$\frac{45000-38000}{1.27-2.41} = \text{slope}$$
$$\frac{7000}{-1.14} = \text{slope}$$

This means that every increase in price of $1.14 decreases demand by 7000.

To write the equation, we can plug one of our points as well as the slope into an expression.

This is how we find the y-intercept of the line:

$$y = (\text{slope})x + \text{intercept}$$
$$45{,}000 = \frac{7000}{-1.14}(1.27) + \text{intercept}$$
$$45{,}000 = -7798.25 + \text{intercept}$$
$$52798.25 = \text{intercept}$$

We have an intercept of 52,798.25. That means that if $x=0$, and sprockets case $0.00, then there will be a demand for 52798.25 of them.

To find out the price point at which demand will equal 42,500, we just plug that in to our new equation as the y-value:

$$42{,}500 = = \frac{7000}{-1.14}(x) + 52{,}798.25$$

$$-10298.25 = \frac{7000}{-1.14}(x)$$

$$1.68 = x$$

Sprockets should be priced at $1.68 apiece.

Analytical Writing Practice

This chapter provides you with an "Analyze an Issue" prompt and an "Analyze an Argument" prompt. These prompts are directly quoted from the ETS.org published pools of essay topics for the GRE. The entire pool of prompts can be found at this URL under "Published Topic Pools for the Analytical Writing Measure":
http://www.ets.org/gre/revised_general/prepare/analytical_writing/

To practice the Analytical Writing task, you should approach these prompts as you would the GRE. Time yourself for each prompt. You are allotted 30 minutes per essay. Your time should begin as soon as you read the essay prompt, so do not read further until you're prepared to start writing your first essay. You can use scratch paper to plan, but you may want to try typing your essay into a word processor to mimic the conditions of the test. Try to use a typing platform that will not autocorrect your spelling, grammar, and capitalization, as these tools will not be available to you on the GRE.

After you've written your essays, see the example essays for each topic to get a sense of what a high-scoring essay would look like. A guideline for scoring your own essay is provided along with the examples.

The Analyze an Issue prompt is presented on the next page.

Analyze an Issue

You have 30 minutes to plan and write your response to the following prompt:

"A nation should require all of its students to study the same national curriculum until they enter college."

Write a response in which you discuss the extent to which you agree or disagree with the statement and explain your reasoning for the position you take. In developing and supporting your position, you should consider ways in which the statement might or might not hold true and explain how these considerations shape your position.[3]

---

[3] Source: ETS.org Pool of Analyze an Issue topics

Analyze an Argument

You have 30 minutes to plan and write your response to the following prompt:

"Twenty years ago, Dr. Field, a noted anthropologist, visited the island of Tertia. Using an observation-centered approach to studying Tertian culture, he concluded from his observations that children in Tertia were reared by an entire village rather than by their own biological parents. Recently another anthropologist, Dr. Karp, visited the group of islands that includes Tertia and used the interview-centered method to study child-rearing practices. In the interviews that Dr. Karp conducted with children living in this group of islands, the children spent much more time talking about their biological parents than about other adults in the village. Dr. Karp decided that Dr. Field's conclusion about Tertian village culture must be invalid. Some anthropologists recommend that to obtain accurate information on Tertian child-rearing practices, future research on the subject should be conducted via the interview-centered method."

Write a response in which you discuss what questions would need to be answered in order to decide whether the recommendation and the argument on which it is based are reasonable.

Be sure to explain how the answers to these questions would help to evaluate the recommendation.[4]

---

[4] Source: ETS.org Pool of Analyze an Issue topics

Analytical Writing Essay Examples

This section provides a scoring guide and an example of a high-scoring essay for each of the essay topics given in the Analytical Writing Practice section. These essays are just examples – the essay you wrote in response to each prompt could take an entirely different approach to the prompt and still score just as highly. Use these essays to get a sense of the general quality of reasoning and prose that is expected of a GRE essay response.

Essay Scoring Guide	
Score	**Description**
6	The essay takes a "clear and insightful position" according to the ETS. The essay is organized and has a logical flow of ideas. The writing is clear and easily understood, with some stylistic variety. Errors are minimal and do not impair the clarity of the essay. The argument is supported with different examples or reasons.
5	The essay takes a thoughtful position. The essay demonstrates logical thinking and organization. Arguments are supported with examples and reasons. The writing is clear and easily understood, with some variety. The difference between a 5 and a 6 seems to be that a 5 is technically proficient but a little less persuasive and inspired than a 6.
4	The essay takes a position on the prompt. The essay demonstrates a logical approach, but organization of the thinking might be less evident. The argument is supported with reasoning and/or examples. The writing is reasonably proficient, but some errors might impede clarity and there may be a lack of variety in the language.
3	The essay does not take a clear position with regard to the topic. The essay may not be clearly organized. The argument is not well-supported with reasoning or examples. Errors in grammar or spelling may obscure some meaning.
2	The essay does not follow the specific instructions in the prompt. The essay does not develop a clear position regarding the prompt. The writing is not organized or particularly logical. Errors in grammar or spelling obscure the meaning.
1	The essay does not adequately answer the prompt. No understanding of developing an argument is demonstrated. The essay may be very short – only a few sentences. Errors in grammar or spelling make the essay difficult to read.
0 or NS	The essay is scored with a 0 if it is entirely off topic, and it is Not scored if it is left blank.

Remember that the two types of essays only differ in one way: Issue Essays place an emphasis on the writer developing a clear position on the topic; Argument Essays, on the other hand, emphasize the writer's ability to clearly identify the position taken within the argument. All other points about reasoning, logic, organization, and coherence are the same; and the essays are graded on the same scale.

Note that an essay does not need to exhibit every trait given in the scoring guide to receive a particular score. Rather, the scoring is done holistically with these guidelines in place. See the Introduction of this guide for more information on the essay scoring process which ETS uses.

Example essay – Analyze an Issue
Proponents of a standard national K-12 curriculum argue that standardizing education is the best way to ensure a quality education for all children growing up in a nation. What they fail to realize is that one size does not fit all when it comes to learning; students need the opportunity to seek a curriculum that excites them and best fits their learning style. Denying students this, particularly at the secondary level, is the way to ensure a mediocre education for all.

Identifying the skills students need to learn in the early grades is easy. Before they can more on to more abstract and specific knowledge, students need to develop literacy and numeracy. Child development experts could develop a universal curriculum to address early-learning needs, and implementing this may be a way to ensure that every child, nationally, is given the foundation for a successful education. However, once students have mastered the basics, what constitutes a "successful education" can no longer be universally prescribed. It was once de rigueur for students to memorize long passages of classical poetry and literature. In our times, we've rejected the recitation requirement in favor of an emphasis on the pursuit of many isolated subjects and proficiency on standardized exams. It is clear that what is considered a "best" education is subject to didactic trends. Rather than subject all students to the curriculum deemed best at this moment, a nation should allow students to determine their own academic paths and give them full support to do so.

People learn best when they are given the opportunity to find and passionately pursue the thing which thrills them. Four fifteen-year-old girls recently won acclaim at an engineering fair in Lagos, Nigeria for developing an electricity generator which runs on hydrogen extracted from urine. Another adolescent girl has recently been named the first African-American female chess master. These young girls, and many other students like them, are taking advantage of special programs at their schools that allow them to delve into science, strategy, project-driven learning, the arts, and many other specialized pursuits. My most memorable moments of learning in high school came not in my subject-driven classes but in an experimental elective course that allowed students to construct an independent project. Friends of mine wrote plays, recorded albums, and filmed short movies, each learning about constructing narratives, time and project management, and a technical field. I followed a passion of mine and conducted my very first large-scale research project on resource mining in the Democratic Republic of the Congo. Given the freedom, I found a mentor at a local university and learned how to find information for myself.

Giving students opportunities like the one I had in secondary school also creates advantages for them later in the education system and the workplace. I arrived at college already knowing that I was passionate about resource distribution issues and with a skill set that included managing my own learning. A nation needs to empower its students early in their education to figure out what they want to know and how they can go about learning that subject. If students follow a regimented program that accounts for every minute of their time in institutionalized learning situations, they'll never develop the desire and the skills to manage their own curiosities.

Advocates of a national curriculum fear that students will fall behind in schools that do not hold them to rigorous academic standards. This would be better addressed through providing support for schools to develop unique programs, and giving students enough information that they can choose the course of study that most appeals to them. Students should not arrive at college having never been asked what they want to learn. Our secondary education system should provide students with opportunities to experiment, test their capabilities, and truly think about and explore what inspires them.

Example Essay – Analyze an Argument

There is not currently sufficient information to determine whether an interview-based research approach is superior to an observation-based approach in drawing conclusions about the child-rearing customs in a culture. To evaluate the merits of each approach, we need to know more about the methodologies used by each anthropologist and about the reaction of the subjects to each very different type of intrusion. The proposal to favor one type of research over another simply because it is more recent is faulty and premature. To further analyze this issue, the anthropology community must weigh the advantages and drawbacks of each method and consider the context.

There are several potential issues with an interview-centered approach to studying a culture from an outside perspective. It is possible that the Tertians were confused by the way Dr. Karp asked the questions, or that some of the people interviewed did not value the anthropologist's research enough to be candid. Often, subjects of interview-centered research need to feel invested in the work being done for the project to be successful, since such a burden of information is placed on their shoulders. This is compounded when the subjects of research are children. These children may not have understood what was being asked, due to the researcher failing to frame questions in age- and culturally-appropriate terms. The children may not have cared about the research, and simply said what they thought Dr. Karp wanted to hear in order to please him or hurry along the interview. This level of engagement is hard to evaluate without audio or video evidence of the interview.

This leads to a second criticism of the interview-centered method: it is possible that Dr. Karp asked questions that led children to focus on their biological parents. All that is known is that the children spent more time speaking of their parents than of other adults in the community. This would be the logical outcome if Dr. Karp asked them questions that prompted them to speak of their parents. To know if the children spontaneously mentioned their parents or if they were led to the topic we would need transcripts of the interviews. As an outsider, it is likely that Dr. Karp inadvertently injected his own assumptions and cultural values while speaking with the children. If Dr. Karp is from a Western culture, then he probably expected biological parents to play a great role in child-rearing and his line of questioning might have reflected that. This is a mistake available to even the most experienced cultural researcher, and to eliminate this possibility of bias we must again consult transcripts of the interviews.

Conversely, there may be advantages to the observation-based protocol that are not recognized by those proposing this interview-based approach. Was Dr. Field permitted to observe the Tertian communities in intimate settings, where social roles would be clearly exhibited? Were the Tertians comfortable around him, and is their culture generally accepting enough of outsiders to allow observation of the people acting normally? Because children are cognitively less developed than adults and have difficulty expressing abstract ideas, more is gained by observing how they react to situations than by asking them to reflect on something like social ties and who is "raising" them. Seeing their lives happen in context might better enable an anthropologist to draw accurate conclusions. To know the validity of Dr. Field's conclusions, it is necessary that we better understand his relationship with the people in the community he studied.

There are drawbacks to both approaches, and a thoughtful anthropology community will recognize the roles that methodology and the researcher's relationship to the subjects play in drawing accurate conclusions about a culture. Perhaps the worst assumption made in this proposal is that only one method is best for obtaining information about the Tertian and other cultures. A hybrid approach might be based; that way researchers can observe interactions happening naturally, and then can question both children and adults in the community about what those interactions meant to them.

Navigating the Electronic GRE

This section will let you know what to expect from the electronic test. A few basic tools are available on the Electronic GRE interface which you ought to understand. For the most part, the interface is easy to navigate.

Each section is preceded by a directions screen. The clock does not start until you move on from this directions screen, so you can take your time to read it. You can access the directions again from within the section, so don't worry about making notes on the directions; but remember! If you go back to the directions screen from within the section, your clock will keep running.

Tools available on every section:

Clock
The clock will display in the upper right-hand corner, counting down through your section time. It's helpful to know how much time you have left, but if the clock is stressing you out, you can select "Hide time" next to the clock. When you have only five minutes left, the clock will flash a few times and display without the option to hide.

Help
Clicking the Help button will take you to a different screen with many tabs with direction for: that particular section, the general test, and specific questions. The question-level directions are related to the question format, such as how to select an answer choice and how many choices you may select. There won't be any content-level help. The clock continues to run while you are in the Help menu. You can click the Return button to exit the Help screen.

In the Quantitative Reasoning section, the Help menu also has a tab describing the different functions of the in-test calculator. We'll cover those in this appendix, but if you forget, you can always check back to that Help tab to clarify how the calculator works.

Quit
This button exits the test and cancels your score. This button is for emergencies only. Don't fret about clicking it accidentally; it will take you to a screen asking "are you sure?" before actually aborting the test.

Exit Section
Clicking this button will end your time in the section prematurely. There's no reason to do this. The only exception is if you are in the final experimental section and you know that it will not be scored (this will be explicit in the directions if you are given an experimental section). If you finish all the questions early, go back to those you were less sure about and check your work, or at least use the extra time to take a mental break. Exiting the Section will whisk you right into the next section.

The Analytical Writing section
First, you will see a directions screen. Once you've read the directions and clicked the Continue button, you will see the prompt. Once the prompt is displayed, the 30-minute clock

begins to count down. Your prompt and the directions will always be displayed in a panel on the left side of the screen. On the right side of the screen is your text editor, where you will write your essay.

You have a few basic tools available in the text editor: Cut, Paste, Undo, and Redo. There is no autocorrect, so those of you who are used to typing without worrying about capitalization or proper punctuation might want to practice for a while with your autocorrect turned off. A few errors here and there will not affect your essay score, but if it looks too sloppy that can detract from your score.

You can use the text box however you want – you can do your outlining and planning in the box and then move sentences around to fit in the final essay. If you do this, just be mindful of the clock and give yourself a few minutes to clean up any sentence fragments or leftover brainstorm words. Or, you can plan on your scratch paper and use the text box only for typing out your essay.

The text box will scroll down to accommodate however much you wish to type. There's no length limit on the essay.

The Verbal and Quantitative Reasoning sections

Question Display
A few features are specific to the multiple-choice format of these sections. First of all, be prepared for the display: only one question given at a time. This is great, because it allow you to focus on only that question. Sometimes multiple questions in a row will draw on the same passage or figure. When this happens, you'll get a split screen: the right side of the screen will display a passage and the left side will change to display one question at a time.

In the Quantitative sections, the top of the screen will display the figure while the bottom half of the screen changes to display one question at a time.

Back and Next
These buttons navigate from question to question in sequential order. Easy!

Mark
Hitting the Mark button will record the question you are on as "marked." When you go to the Review screen, you'll be able to see all the questions you've marked. Different people have different ways of using the Mark button. You can Mark a question that you've answered but are unsure of and want to check if you have extra time, or you can Mark a question if it seems like it will take too long to answer and you want to maybe go back to it later. Many people don't use the Mark function at all. A Mark has no effect on your question score.

Review

The Review button will take you to a special screen within a section. The clock does not stop running when you visit the Review screen. All the Review screen gives you is a chart. The chart looks like this:

Question Number	Status	Marked
1	Answered	
2	Not Answered	
3	Incomplete	✔
4	Not Seen	

The Review table will display a row for every question in the section. Questions you have marked will have a check next to them. Here's a code for the different statuses possible for each question:

- **Answered** – you have recorded a full response for the question.

- **Not answered** – you have recorded no response.

- **Incomplete** – you have partially answered the question. This only refers to Text Completion questions with multiple blanks. "Select all that apply" questions will not notify you if you have not selected enough answer choices, because that would give too much away.

- **Not seen** – you have not yet visited the screen with this question on it.

The Review screen is helpful for making sure that you've answered all the questions in a section. You should visit it once you've been through the whole section to check that you haven't skipped over something. You want every question to be recorded as "Answered." Remember, there's no penalty for answering a question incorrectly.

From the Review screen, you can select a specific question and click "Go to Question." If you click "Return," you will go back to the last question you were on before you went to the Review screen.

The Calculator

In the Quantitative Reasoning section, there is a button to bring up the Calculator. Once the Calculator is displayed, it will stay up from question to question unless you close it with the X button in the top right corner. It looks like this:

170

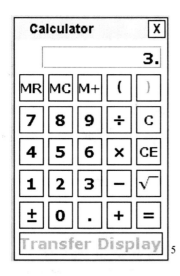

The Calculator functions are pretty simple:

M+ Adds the number on the screen to the calculator memory
MR Recalls the number which is stored in the memory
MC Clears the number stored in the memory
C Clears the entire expression you've entered
CE Clears the last number entered ("clear entry")
Transfer Display

If you are answering a text-box problem, clicking this button will transfer the number displayed in your calculator to the text box in a correct answer format.

The rest of the functions are similar to those on every basic calculator: add, multiply, subtract, divide, and square root. The ± button will change your entered number to a positive or negative number.

The calculator respects Order of Operations, so if you type in "1 + 4 x 5 =" it will perform the multiplication first.

It's best, however, not to rely on the calculator for all of your algebra. Work things out on paper and check each step. Hurrying and relying on the calculator can result in many errors.

The Help screen has a tab explaining the functions of the calculator, in case you forget, but remember that the clock does NOT stop running when you visit the Help screen.

You won't have any graphing functions, but you won't need them. Remember, you are given all the tools you need to answer each question correctly.

Examples of working problems out with the on-screen calculator can be found here:
http://www.ets.org/gre/revised_general/prepare/quantitative_reasoning/calculator/

---

[5] Source: ETS POWERPREP II software

Free Additional Resources

There are many strategy blogs, practice materials, and other additional resources available to you online if you want to prepare further. However, you should be wary of wasting your time on a resource that may be misinformed. The GRE was overhauled in 2011, and there are a lot of guides still available that focus on aspects of the GRE that no longer exist such as: analogies and question-level adaptivity, as well as different question and section formats. Don't get confused by looking at out-of-date resources. For this reason, we recommend the ETS.org resources outlined below and the Khan Academy for brushing up on specific concepts.

The ETS Website
Your best online resource for all things GRE is to go straight to the source of the test. The Educational Testing Service, creator and arbiter of the GRE, maintains a lot of resources and information on their website: www.ets.org/gre. This is the site where you will need to set up a (free) account to register for the test, find testing locations, and manage your score reports.

Also found on the ETS site:
- A full-length paper practice GRE.
- Free software download of POWERPREP II.
- Strategies and tips.
- A very comprehensive FAQ.
- The entire pool of possible essay topics.
- A defensive page detailing all the ways that the GRE can be considered "fair and valid."

The strategies and tips presented on the ETS site are much less direct than what you find in this Accepted, Inc. guide. However, if you have any lingering questions, the ETS site is probably the best place for you to start looking for answers.

Essay Pools
The pool of essay topics is helpful to skim to get a general idea of the types of questions that will be presented to you on your GRE test, but the list is far too long to attempt to prepare for each topic specifically. Please don't try to do that – you'll confuse yourself and get essay burnout. The essay topic pools can be found here:
- Analyze an Issue:
  http://www.ets.org/gre/revised_general/prepare/analytical_writing/issue/pool
- Analyze an Argument:
  http://www.ets.org/gre/revised_general/prepare/analytical_writing/argument/pool

PowerPrep II
ETS's POWERPREP II is an excellent tool for GRE preparation. It includes a sandbox-style "test prep" environment to allow you to build familiarity with the format of the online test, and two full timed and scored online practice tests. The software is only available for Windows. If you want to get a good feel for the electronic format, we recommend that you

check this tool out. It's unnecessary to take both tests; maybe try taking one of each section type.

PowerPrep can be found here:
http://www.ets.org/gre/revised_general/prepare/powerprep2/download

You can find similar electronic test simulators to run on a Mac operating system, but you will likely have to pay to download them.

Khan Academy

If there are specific math topics that you feel you need further practice on, Khan Academy is an excellent resource: www.khanacademy.org. The Arithmetic and Pre-Algebra, Algebra, and Geometry sub-sections should cover everything you need. Remember, the GRE does not test on more advanced math, so don't spent time and intellectual energy cramming more math topics than you'll actually need before the test. Of course, Khan Academy is a rabbit hole of interesting knowledge…but save your exploration of differential equations for *after* you've taken the GRE.

Final Thoughts

In the end, we know that you will be successful in taking the GRE. Although the road ahead may at times be challenging, if you continue your hard work and dedication (just like you are doing to prepare for the GRE), you will find that your efforts will pay off.

If you are struggling after reading this book and following our guidelines, we sincerely hope that you will take note of our advice and seek additional help. Start by asking friends about the resources that they are using. If you are still not reaching the score you want, consider getting the help of a GRE tutor.

If you are on a budget and cannot afford a private tutoring service, there are plenty of independent tutors, including college students who are proficient in GRE subjects. You don't have to spend thousands of dollars to afford a good tutor or review course.

We wish you the best of luck and happy studying. Most importantly, we hope you enjoy your coming years – after all, you put a lot of work into getting there in the first place.

Sincerely,

The Accepted, Inc. Team

STUDY SMARTER. SCORE HIGHER. GET ACCEPTED.

CPSIA information can be obtained at www.ICGtesting.com
Printed in the USA
BVOW04s1852280814

364705BV00009B/128/P